LET'S WORK SMARTER, NOT HARDER

Also available from ASQ Quality Press

The Change Agents' Handbook: A Survival Guide for Quality Improvement Champions
David W. Hutton

Quality Quotes
Hélio Gomes

Insights to Performance Excellence 1997: An Inside Look at the 1997 Baldrige Award Criteria
Mark L. Blazey

Mapping Work Processes
Dianne Galloway

Measuring and Managing Customer Satisfaction: Going for the Gold
Sheila Kessler

Business Process Benchmarking: Finding and Implementing Best Practices
Robert C. Camp

The Quality Toolbox
Nancy R. Tague

To request a complimentary catalog of publications, call 800-248-1946.

LET'S WORK SMARTER, NOT HARDER

How to Engage Your Entire Organization in the Execution of Change

Michael Caravatta

ASQ Quality Press
Milwaukee, Wisconsin

Let's Work Smarter, Not Harder
How to Engage Your Entire Organization in the Execution of Change
Michael Caravatta

Library of Congress Cataloging-in-Publication Data
Caravatta, Michael, 1940–
    Let's work smarter, not harder: how to engage your entire
organization in the execution of change / Michael Caravatta.
        p.   cm.
    Includes bibliographical references and index.
    ISBN 0-87389-386-7 (alk. paper)
        1. Organizational change.   2. Leadership.   3. Teams in the
    workplace.   I. Title.
HD58.8.C353   1997
658.4'06—dc21   97-3241
                                                          CIP

10 9 8 7 6 5 4 3 2 1

ISBN 0-87389-386-7

Acquisitions Editor: Roger Holloway
Project Editor: Jeanne W. Bohn

ASQ Mission: To facilitate continuous improvement and increase customer satisfaction by identifying, communicating, and promoting the use of quality principles, concepts, and technologies; and thereby be recognized throughout the world as the leading authority on, and champion for, quality.

Attention: Schools and Corporations
ASQ Quality Press books, videotapes, audiotapes, and software are available at quantity discounts with bulk purchases for business, educational, or instructional use. For information, please contact ASQ Quality Press at 800-248-1946, or write to ASQ Quality Press, P.O. Box 3005, Milwaukee, WI 53201-3005.

For a free copy of the ASQ Quality Press Publications Catalog, including ASQ membership information, call 800-248-1946.

Printed in the United States of America

 Printed on acid-free paper

American Society for Quality

Quality Press
611 East Wisconsin Avenue
Milwaukee, Wisconsin 53202

This book is dedicated to my mother, Eleanor.
Throughout her life she put her children before others.
As I look back, she inspired me to rise to
levels of achievement I never dreamed possible.
I wish I could have done more for her.

CONTENTS

  Aim of This Chapter
  Management Leadership Is Required
  Senior Management Must Establish a Business System
  Leadership's Role Is Fourfold
  Senior Management Must Have Its Priorities in the Right Place
  Differences in Management Focus
  Management Must Create a Culture of Innovation and Improvement
  Going Around in Circles
  Where Are You?
  Does Your Management Style Need Changing?
  Paradigms Must Change
  Commitment to a New Way
  Concepts of Process Control

PREFACE

Past success is just that. In today's rapidly changing business environment, survival depends on lean-and-mean operations. You can no longer depend on business as usual. Shorter product life cycles, market deregulation, and global competition have created an ever-changing environment. We know that enormous technological advances have changed everyone's roles dramatically, overwhelming many with the maelstrom of required change. In fact, an organization's ability to change is often a make-or-break proposition in today's competitive marketplace.

Leading change is a most difficult challenge. It may seem threatening, but it also provides opportunities. Will your business be leading the pack or lagging behind the competition—innovating or imitating? What will your customers expect? Do you have a strategy for executing successful change? These are tough questions, but ones you must ask yourself as the intensity of change escalates.

No single issue is capable of producing a more profound influence on the ability of organizations to improve productivity and reduce costs than executing successful change. Without change, little is attainable. Shrinking throughput in less than three months by at least 30 percent to 100 percent is relatively easy without adding resources once you understand how to do it.

Businesses all over the world are trying to improve their competitive positions. Many of these efforts will either fail or be short-lived because of the execution techniques used. *How to excel at executing successful change is what this book is all about.* Making good businesses better and successful businesses superior often demands a shift in existing paradigms.

Organizational change reconstructs the power and influence of a business—not only modifying how people work, but how performance is measured. Changes that are often subtle, sometimes seemingly simple, save millions of dollars. Every once in a while you must stop and ask yourself, "Why are we doing it this way?" In my book you will first absorb the methods and then follow through with successful execution. Every business or organization can use my methods to engage its workforce. *Let's Work Smarter, Not Harder* will show you how to meet customer expectations and remove non–value-adding activities.

The book can be explained with an old Chinese story. A beggar asked a young boy for one of the fish he had just caught. The boy turned to his father and asked if it was okay to give the beggar one. The father replied, "If you give him a fish, you will satisfy his hunger today. If you teach him how to fish, you will satisfy his hunger for life." *Let's Work Smarter, Not Harder* teaches readers how to fish. The book's job is like that of the young boy: teaching readers how to execute successful change in what they do every day.

These methods for change were developed, implemented, and proven in services and manufacturing areas over a period of seven years in the manufacture of electronics, integrated circuits, circuit board fabrication, plastics, metals, and printing, as well as in services including treasury operations, finance and accounting, payroll, facilities, security services, traffic, export services, customer service, field service, human resources, marketing, engineering, purchasing, and systems support. By removing a nickel's worth of this or a dime's worth of that, many times changes are so small that they go unnoticed. They can amount to thousands of dollars in savings over a year's time.

Change must entail senior management's participation and the hard work of many, as well as innovation and creativity, to change the status quo. Executing the disciplines of change requires that managers and employees rethink what they do. They must focus together on customer needs and fulfillment speed. Time is money.

Time consumption is quantifiable; its velocity can be measured and therefore must be managed. Radical change is possible; manufacturing processes can shrink from 110 days to 3 days, and end-of-month closings in accounting can shrink from 28 days to 2 days. It isn't rocket science; my proven methods and techniques are provided in a sound, common-sense way, complete with detailed explanations and examples of techniques to be used.

Businesses will no longer continue to exist if they don't learn to change the way customer value is delivered. It starts with the way a business thinks about itself: its organizational philosophy, communications, visions, missions, process flows, and response time to internal and external customers.

Careful manipulation of internal processes—coordinating, rearranging, simplifying—requires the skills of all employees working together and gaining insights into how to improve their effectiveness as change agents. Workers understand the intimate details of the organization and new employees examine with new eyes, ideas, and thoughts. Involve everyone in rethinking your business through change. Rethinking leads to improved productivity and process ownership by identifying processes that aren't productive or are slow to respond. It eliminates redundant movements, wasteful materials, and activities without harmful side effects on other actions.

The rewards are yours. Starting is half the battle. Executing successful change is where most organizations go wrong. Here is a rigorous approach to execute and change the status quo: bridging the gap between thinking about change and successful execution, filling the big gap in the middle. How long will it take you to achieve world-class operations? You'll either decide to start in the next few seconds—or you may procrastinate. Don't cripple your business.

INTENDED AUDIENCE

Those that have responsibility for executing successful change in their organizations to compete in the next century are primary targets for this book. Everyone discusses change, but no one has written really good guidelines on *how to execute change.* This book was written as a guide to assist second-level and frontline managers and their workforce to execute successful change in administration, service, and manufacturing functions. Methods are equally applicable to all areas; this is a single execution methodology.

The book is also useful for senior managers who are interested in learning more about changing their businesses. Even those that are experienced in making change happen will benefit from the book.

Secondary targets include human resource professionals, college professors, and business school professors using the book as a text for how to execute paradigmatic change in organizational structure.

ACKNOWLEDGMENTS

Special thanks go to Gina Eastman for editing grammar and sentence structure. I am also indebted to Paul Bachelor (Supplier Business Manager, Sequent Computer Systems), Ken Choi (President of K.C. International), Tim Dedlow (Oregon State Quality Award Program Manager), Jerry Folmar (Vice President of Corporate Quality Assurance, Griffith Rubber Mills), Thomas Krueger (Manager of Economic Development, Portland General Electric), Mike Wright (Director of Operations, IMG, Inc.), Neil Isenberg (Operations Manager, AMC, Inc.), Bill Peterson, and Carl Schuetze for their supportive peer reviews.

This book is the result of much generous assistance, advice, support, and encouragement given to me by many friends and business associates. I thankfully acknowledge the many contributions of clients whose vivacious experimenting provided real-world examples that made my text come alive. When referring to my clients and me working together I use the term *we* in the text. If it were not for them, there would be no book.

It is important to state that my basic work on building shared vision and improving daily work processes started in the mid-1980s when I was with Tektronix, Inc. in Wilsonville, Oregon. This book expands on this original work and reflects five years of successfully applying these basic concepts to other businesses and organizations.

INTRODUCTION

IF YOUR BUSINESS IS SUCCESSFUL, WHY CHANGE?

People in businesses and organizations often ask why they should spend time and effort to improve productivity when they are doing very well today. First of all, there are almost always hidden profits in any organization just waiting to be recovered from inefficient policy deployment and processes. Second, the competition is not idly sitting by while your business remains at status quo.

To avoid this predicament you can start recovering lost profits by adopting a mind-set of focusing on streamlining business and daily work processes and preventing errors that add no value. This may sound like plain common sense, but we have found that a policy of continually reviewing and improving productivity is still alien to far too many businesses. Consider the following reasons why you should start improving productivity to reduce your business costs now.

1. *It is less costly to reduce the cost of doing business than it is to increase sales volume.** The circulation of capital in any business is

---

*Excerpted by permission of the publisher, from *Consultative Selling* 5E. © 1985 Mack Hanan. Published by AMACOM, a division of American Management Association. All rights reserved.

directly related to the time it takes to secure, use, and replenish it (that is, cash is converted into inventories, sales, and receivables, minus overhead expenses; the remaining cash then starts the cycle over again). The faster this conversion takes place, the greater your profits will be.

In his book *Consultative Selling*, Mack Hanan (1985) discusses three ways to increase capital turnover rates: (1) decrease operating costs (processes and overhead); (2) increase sales volume; or (3) improve both. Most companies focus on increasing sales, while in fact it is less costly (and there are usually more opportunities) to reduce operating expenses.

Consider the examples illustrated in Figure I.1. A company has yearly sales of $100K and the total capital needed to conduct business is $100K. One rotation cycle of the sales drive gear equals a total capital turnover of 100 percent, with working funds turning over twice as fast, or 200 percent annually. (The sales and total capital gears rotate in proportion to their size.)

To increase capital turnover, this company could increase sales for the year to $200K; total capital turnover would now increase to 200 percent and working funds turnover would increase to 400 percent annually. In this scenario, all operating funds are being worked harder.

Alternatively, the company could improve business processes and reduce total operating capital required, yet still maintain the same increased turnover in both total capital and working funds. There are more opportunities in most companies to reduce capital (overhead) expenses by 5 percent than there are to increase sales volume by 25 percent. Figure I.1 (bottom) shows that increasing sales earnings can cost 10 times more than reducing operating capital for the same turnover.

Use of capital is directly proportional to reduced process through-put time within your company. The reduction of capital (overhead) expenses through productivity improvements should be a primary goal of all businesses.

2. *Competition is increasing.* Competitors, specifically on the Asian Rim, are moving more and more into U.S. businesses and industries (for example, banking, heavy industries, automotive, television and VCR production, retail businesses, movie and recording studios, sporting

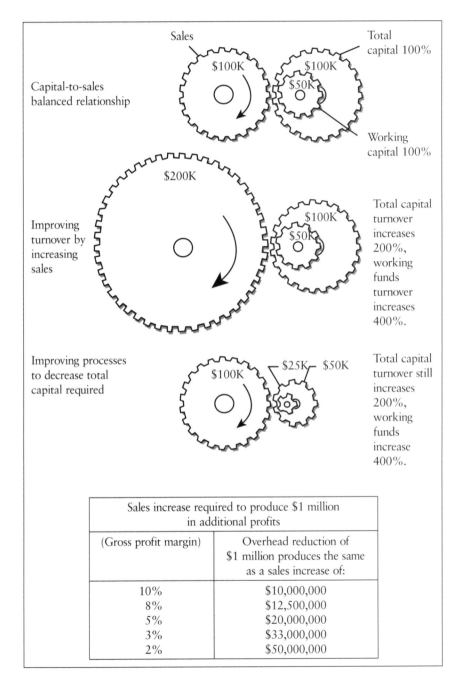

Figure I.1. Capital-to-sales relationship.

equipment, and administrative and service businesses). A key reason for their continual success in penetrating world markets is that their cost prevention techniques are simply better. They concentrate on every little detail to improve business and daily work processes. Realizing just how good many Asian businesses are at defect prevention and elimination is often a shocking eye-opener for many business owners.

Just how fast productivity improvements need to be made to meet and exceed international competition is a big question, but some startling facts may help put things in perspective. During the 1980s, U.S. manufacturing productivity improved approximately 4.1 percent per year. During the same period, productivity improvements in administration and service sectors registered an average annual increase of only 0.2 percent. For 1995, manufacturing productivity increased at 4.0 percent. Overall productivity improvement of all economic sectors has averaged 1 percent per year (1994 was 0.7 percent, and 1995 was 0.9 percent per the U.S. Bureau of Labor Statistics). Will improvement sustained at this rate improve U.S. competitiveness and reduce the trade imbalance? No way! If we continue to maintain this rate, most businesses will either be severely challenged or their markets will be taken over by competitors. During the next 20 years, vast improvements in productivity are projected for Italy, France, Germany, and specifically the Asian Rim countries of Japan and Korea (Annual Productivity Survey 1991).

3. *The government will not help you keep your business competitive.* There was a time when American businesses had minimal international competition and were protected somewhat by various governmental trade laws. This is no longer the case. U.S. businesses today are an integral part of the global market economy and should not wait until they are threatened with extinction before they do something. You must start now to involve all individuals in rethinking, suggesting, and implementing methods for lowering costs and errors in daily activities. Everyone in the company must become profit-motivated and continually think about how to improve business productivity and profits. This requires total management and employee participation.

4. *Everyone needs to work and share together; you need teamwork.* Unless all members of your company feel they are participating and have process ownership (responsibility), chances are you will not remain competitive. One method of finding out how well employees work together is to conduct a pronoun test. To do this, ask your employees a few general questions about your quality system, and listen to the words they use. If the answers contain pronouns such as *they* or *them*, your company lacks unity of all departments and the employees within them. They are probably blaming others for existing problems and feedback communications need repair. If the answers contain pronouns such as *we* or *us*, you will know that management leadership has created process teamwork, ownership, and sharing. Even a statement like *they aim for high quality* suggests that the workplace has not achieved a learning and sharing environment. Every person should be responding with *we do this together, our* business is succeeding, or *we* are improving and becoming better every day.

5. *You need a high-performance, high value-adding workplace.* In a highly productive and profitable workplace, all personnel from the bottom up are constantly looking for ways to prevent errors and simplify processes to cut costs. The advantage a *we* business has is that *everyone* looks for, discovers, and learns new ways to improve total process costs that serve internal or external customers. In a *we* organization, you often cannot distinguish managers from other employees. In a high-performance work environment everyone works together, communicates together, learns together, and prospers together. Workers must become more knowledgeable of all facets of the business.

With that in mind, the old top-down management approach becomes weaker and weaker in the face of increasing competition. Employees need the freedom to rethink and fix or prevent errors without seeking case-by-case approval. The new competitive advantage comes in the form of being flexible and responsive and in using whatever learning methods, technologies, and resources are required to meet the specific needs of customers.

In a high-performance workplace, knowledgeable employees feel responsible for their company's future—they know that they will make the business succeed or fail. In a broader sense, employees feel that they own the company—they make up its most important assets, they collectively assist in making most of the important day-to-day decisions, and they do well when the company does well.

ATTAINING HIGH PERFORMANCE REQUIRES EMPOWERING THE WORKFORCE

In brief, empowerment is authorizing employees (giving responsibility) at the lowest levels possible to make decisions and take necessary actions to prevent errors. Realizing that the knowledge and creative abilities of employees can greatly enhance the success of their business, managers must adapt a style that includes employees in the decision-making process and emphasizes teamwork. Empowering employees with the will to perform their best will accomplish this goal.

Often the difference between empowering and delegating is misunderstood. *Delegating* is authorizing others to act for you, while *empowering* provides the authority (responsibility) to take the actions necessary to prevent problems as well as to make decisions. There is no empowerment if decisions that affect employees are made for them by management and employees are only given the responsibility to implement others' decisions.

Managers must learn to function more as coaches—training others to be self-directed and to work well with others. Once employees begin making some of their own decisions, a manager becomes just another team player. The undesirable management-by-crisis syndrome will become a thing of the past because employees will brainstorm their way out of problem situations as they occur. *Management's failure to delegate, let alone empower (give responsibility to) employees, is the foundation for many of today's business headaches.*

Implementing a management style that emphasizes teamwork and shared leadership can be very challenging. Many times management itself is the biggest obstacle to developing a creative, responsible, and knowledgeable workplace. Breaking traditional habits of overseeing everything, following chains of command, maintaining the same organizational structure, and hoarding information is difficult. Managers must examine how they may unintentionally be preventing employee empowerment.

When empowering employees, managers often run into a real dilemma. Managers tell employees they're empowered—but they still keep asking for authorization to do things, feeling they're not adequately prepared to make decisions and the necessary changes. It all comes down to the question of how comfortable they feel to implement the change. They need to be educated and trained in the latest improvement methodologies. These include the following:

- Activity-based costing
- Continuous improvement in daily work
- Cross-functional process management
- Teamwork and employee involvement
- The five Ss for good housekeeping
- Visual methods for improving process performance
- Benchmarking
- Building shared vision
- Effective listening
- Empowerment
- Total quality management

Another impediment is the reluctance of many top executives to give up control (share power) and to entrust employees with daily process decisions. You must replace power with responsibility. Most executives are in their position because they are good at exerting authority and control. Without training, managers who have excelled in the old system are usually among the least likely to lead into the new system. Their habitual *we* pronouns often do not include the employees.

■ ■ ■

The *Association for Quality and Participation Newsletter,* December/January 1996, discusses the results of a survey conducted in 1993 by the University of Southern California School of Business Administration's Center for Effective Organizations. A 16-page questionnaire was sent to 985 companies from the 1992 Fortune 1000 list of the nation's 1000 largest manufacturing and service companies. Two hundred seventy-nine companies responded to the survey. Their responses indicated that

- 37 percent of employees do not participate in employee involvement activities and have no share in managerial power.

- 31 percent of employees are responsible for recommending improvements to management, but they have no power and get little information or training to help them make decisions.

- 12 percent of employees participate in teams given some degree of control over the day-to-day decisions relevant to their jobs, but they only receive information directly related to their tasks.

- Only 10 percent of employees are heavily involved in business management, receiving extensive training in group dynamics and getting information on the business's overall performance, especially as it relates to competitors.

■ ■ ■

EXECUTING CHANGE IN AN ORGANIZED MANNER IS NOT EASY

Organizations will usually find it difficult to change their culture when moving from managing people to managing processes. Cultural change requires adjustments to the way things are currently being done—the way managers manage, the way employees work together, the way they communicate with each other, the way they learn together, and the way customers' needs are fulfilled. Change requires much thought and the empowerment of all participants in its execution.

With this realization, however, comes the challenge for senior management: "What should I do to generate effective change within my organization?" When developing a strategy for change, senior managers should first build a foundation of understanding within their organization. Like building a house, you begin with a sound foundation. Part I, Establishing a Foundation, discusses the disciplines (instruction, control) necessary to engage change. Chapter 1, Management Leadership, describes how leaders must guide and stay on the course. Chapter 2, Cross-Functional Business Relationships, will allow you to mandate different organizational structures. Chapter 3, Customer/Supplier Relationships, must be understood; it is important to understand who all your downstream customers are. Chapter 4, Learning Teams, teaches how to use described tools to share knowledge and hold productive learning team meetings.

Once the foundation for change is understood, Part II, Execution: How to Do It! begins explaining the disciplines (analysis, training, instruction, control) used. Chapter 5, Conducting an Organizational Self-Assessment, describes how to self-assess your business to focus on what should be done differently. Hopefully, this includes discussions (soliciting participation) with subordinates, employees, peers, and supervisors to identify both the strengths that can be built on and the weak areas that need improvement. Next follow the steps in chapter 6, Building Shared Vision, to attain participative ownership and management of selected core projects identified in chapter 5. Core project processes must be continuously managed and measured. In chapter 7, Processes: Making Them Come Alive, documented processes become more visible. Chapter 8, Measurements and Feedback, provides tools to ensure that improvement is continuous. Whatever you measure is going to happen, so you had better be measuring the right things. Chapter 9, Continuous Improvement in Daily Work, provides a series of steps that anyone can use to improve daily work tasks. The steps in this chapter are used to document the small, detailed steps in cross-functional core projects. When senior management support for cross-functional process management is not evident, use these steps to improve individual, department, and functional daily work tasks.

Together the two parts provide an excellent framework within which you will improve the performance level of your business or organization, as well as a methodology to develop and integrate strategic plans with daily work processes. You simply must uncover existing non–value-adding activities to find opportunities for improvement before you can do anything about them. Management can then create a strategic vision, missions, goals, and objectives for necessary change and improvement and can create the required mind-set in the associates. Engage your entire organization in the disciplines of change to become not only a little bit better, but a whole lot better.

The glossary will help readers understand how I am using various words and phrases. We have chosen to use some words in a broader context or in a more simplified form.

Part I

ESTABLISHING
A
FOUNDATION

CHAPTER 1

MANAGEMENT LEADERSHIP

AIM OF THIS CHAPTER

This chapter describes the daunting management leadership necessary to execute the methodologies, methods, and changes that are discussed in the body of the book. Adoption of the methodologies requires a new mind-set—a cultural change within the company. Management leadership's mind-set and thinking is the first thing to be changed. Here the focus is on building commitment among managers, selecting correct management styles, updating or developing new leadership roles, and understanding the challenges and opportunities faced. As a leader you must think every day about not becoming complacent. You must work every day at purging people of the notion that everything is fixed.

How to use company employees to increase productivity is unquestionably one of the most challenging management leadership objectives of our time. This chapter discusses how management leadership must establish an ultimately empowered (process-responsible) environment for employees to be effective as contributors, problem solvers, and executors of change. Today there's a big knowledge gap in the middle of most organizations, and knowledge must be shared down to the lowest levels of a business. And if that isn't enough, senior management now has an opportunity to include administration, services, and manufacturing together in total process improvement efforts. You are now charged with building an organization that's responsive, flexible, and agile—able to move faster than your competitors to increase market share and maintain profitability. One thing is certain: Tomorrow's managers, executives, and employees will do things differently.

MANAGEMENT LEADERSHIP IS REQUIRED

What are the qualities of a good leader? How much is inborn, how much can be taught, and how much must be learned through experience? There never has been—and there probably never will be—an all-encompassing list of qualities that apply to all leadership situations. Leadership skills can be acquired through teaching, observing, mentoring, and other life experiences. Some leaders have less to learn, some learn faster, and some never do learn. Each has a unique set of talents, family background, education, interests, career path, and work experience. What does executing change—the job at hand—require? Five leaders may have five different answers to this question.

First and foremost, cultural change requires *good leadership*. Without good leadership, many well-intentioned efforts at change will be stymied. Howard Gardner, in his new book *Leading Minds: An Anatomy of Leadership* (1996), states that leadership is a transition between leaders and followers that supports a common shared vision. Leaders must have followers. When effective leadership occurs, followers take care of themselves. The words of the Chinese philosopher Lao-tsu describe what makes a good leader.

> *A leader is best when people barely know they exist. Not so good when people obey and acclaim them. Worse when they despise them. But of a good leader who talks little, when their work is done and their aim fulfilled, they will say, "We did it ourselves."*

The days of authoritative micromanagement are gone. Managers must cope with the challenges of globalization, horizontal process management, empowerment, and fast-paced technical innovation. The qualities listed as follows will assist managers in leading today's organizations. Leadership can be defined as positive behavior that displays the ability and willingness to accomplish change. You are a good leader when you

- Are able to cope with adversity (be prepared to be uncomfortable) as the company undergoes structural change, either organizationally or in its markets. Good leaders know the change journey never ends.

- Are self-confident and can produce simple plans, speak simply, and propose clear targets that create a boundaryless small-company culture. If people see something that needs to be done, they do it.

- Replace managing, organizing, and controlling with visions, values, and learning teams. You promote change by influencing people's skills, enthusiasm, competitiveness, commitment, trust, and productive behavior to achieve long-term strategic objectives. Leaders must direct their management and employee development efforts toward the creation of learning teams.

- Are not shy about using the V-word: Plan a shared, compelling, articulated *vision* of the future and meticulous planning to work that vision. Today's leaders are playing a demanding, hands-on role, developing the strategic direction of the organization, as well as resolving ongoing operational issues. Employees must have a felt need and sense of purpose. Open up the management and planning process to every employee of the organization. A sense of ownership is a powerful incentive for business change. Conceptualize and articulate understandable goals and visions (guiding ideas) of future activities that people can be emotional about and want to achieve—a vision that translates into a practical execution and an improved or new business, organization, process, job performance, and behavior change. It is clearly difficult to drive the message all the way down in an organization and make sure it is championed by every member of the organization. Power comes from transmitting information and articulating it with one unified set of measurements that include customer and employee satisfaction, internal business processes, finance, and marketshare growth. Set stretch goals and reward performance.

- Present ideas, not mandates, and get out of the way. It encourages people to offer and accept suggestions and ideas to solve customer problems instead of passing problems on to others. You must give employees permission to fail, because failure is a learning tool. When challenging something, ask if it's in the procedure instead of telling someone to do something.

- Manage boundaries and resources.

  —Prevent unnecessary boundary interference by removing communication obstacles that prevent a "supplier" from satisfying a "customer," whether that customer is an internal or external customer.

  —Provide necessary resources, such as staff, training, tools, procedures, and raw materials necessary to complete daily work.

- Demonstrate there is a link between continuous learning and continuous improvement. Place an emphasis on learning from customers what to change. Make sure you understand the service your customers require. Identify high-leverage opportunities for change before your customers do, then focus on executing the changes to exceed their demands.

- Show support to all those below the executive positions through visible means. One way to change your support is to change the way you talk. Power must be in the hands of process owners. Practice MBWA—management by walking around—and talk with workers daily to see what can be removed (or added) to make their jobs easier. (Those companies whose senior management spends up to 20 percent of its time directly on process-related issues are the most successful.)

- Become a good coach, communicator, facilitator, and director, and an outstanding team builder and motivator. Good managers have both a high people and high task orientation. Recognize and reinforce positive employee behavior and performance. Specifically address those issues that require a behavior or performance modification. Putting together a strong and effective management leadership team is tough. You want managers from different disciplines—managers who are committed to your people and to their success. Finding them is not always easy, but the rewards can be immense.

- Create and maintain an environment that fosters creativity and provides the capability to innovate. Growth strategies must have innovation at its center. More than creating, innovation involves the ability to change where the organization is headed. Innovation occurs in two ways: autonomously and systematically. Autonomous innovations can be pursued independently from other innovations (they are discussed in chapter 9). Systematic innovations are those that are tied to other related innovations (they are discussed in chapter 2). Real breakthroughs come only when employees realize and admit they have *ownership, accountability, and responsibility* for finding and removing chronic problems in both autonomous and systematic processes.

- Put supply chain management on your priority list (senior management must do this), or the integration of activities won't occur and carry the organization into the twenty-first century. Remember this: You cannot substitute supply chain management for the methods in place today (such as MRP, SPC, JIT, and so on); it must be linked with them to limit organizational turmoil.

- Develop a lasting approach to managing change. We all know that the organization that accepts change will win. Change often requires dramatic mental attitude shifts, information technology, and management expertise. Change is a continuous process. Everyone needs to recognize that it is a long-term commitment—people are the primary source of competitive change. Arm everyone with pride, methods, and measurements (customer satisfaction, internal business processes, finance, and market share growth) for executing strategic change. Motivate your entire workforce to stay alert to opportunities, to work together to implement change, and to pursue sustained growth and profitability.

- Look for big-picture opportunities with a bottom-line orientation toward results that must satisfy customers. Examine what you've been doing, establish new initiatives, measure results, find where you have been having problems, and find out where you need to correct strategic directions.

Managers who have a satisfactory balance of these traits will lead their companies' change into the twenty-first century and beyond. There are some negative traits associated with leadership that must be avoided.

- Misunderstanding the role of management. Don't try to "manage" people—you *build* quality people and *manage* processes. You cannot manage people's performance; you can only create a desire in them for excellence in whatever they do. Build quality people in your organization—people you have trust in and they in you. Would quality people produce or provide shoddy goods or services? Not likely! Would they assume responsibility for themselves and their output? Very likely!

- Being too restrictive—rigid authoritarians thwart learning (merge thinking and actions in every individual to shifting business conditions). Rigid control creates fear; fear is the direct opposite of trust. Let people who perform daily tasks get on with their jobs with minimum interference.

- Taking credit for other's accomplishments (say *we* and *our* instead of *I*).

- Dictating rather than suggesting (lead people to other methods).

- Promoting fear in the organization by inhibiting creativity, openness, trust, and change (create an open, trusting environment—don't shoot the messengers of bad news). The last thing you want to do is use words or statements that can stifle the flow of ideas and cause people to hold back, or give up altogether. Respond to suggestions and innovation with "Until now we've done it this way" and "How can we do it better?" Say, "Let's try it!"

- Most important, failing to support organizational *employee* vision and value statements.

SENIOR MANAGEMENT MUST ESTABLISH A BUSINESS SYSTEM

In a recent address to the Business for Social Responsibility group, a Washington, D.C.–based think tank studying the interrelationships between business and society, Lester Thurow, economics and management guru from MIT, said that in order for Western businesses to be successful they must have a system—more organization, more structured processes, and more training and education. He said a key problem in achieving this is that there is an unwillingness to set and enforce standards of quality, both in education and business.

Process standards are a fundamental element of all businesses' systems and are a necessary base against which to measure improvement. Key processes within the business are people's daily work. This system (the linking of connecting functional daily activities, such as described in the ISO 9000 series system documentation) must be continuously evaluated, improved, and managed if the business or organization is to be competitive. Management must be the catalyst behind a thorough analysis of business and daily work processes—documenting them, analyzing their interrelationships, and continually improving them through the elimination of activities that add no value.

While manufacturing organizations have focused on process improvement strategies since the early 1950s, administration and service groups in most cases have not. We use the terms *administration* and *service* to refer to all those groups within a company, business, or organization that provide a service to other groups, including manufacturing. It is within these groups that most senior management leaders must focus their attention, if they have not yet done so. It has been estimated that 86 percent of all jobs in the global economy are either directly or indirectly associated with administration and service groups within a company or organization. Yet most of the processes associated with these jobs have not been included in management's improvement strategies. Management and employees unfortunately look at administration and service functions differently from manufacturing functions. In one case, only 3 percent of the suggested improvements were for administration and services. Yet administration and service productivity opportunities are abundant and must be attacked with the same intensity and vigor competitors are displaying.

LEADERSHIP'S ROLE IS FOURFOLD

Both domestic and foreign companies generally agree that the overall role of management leadership is fourfold: (1) discover, analyze, lead, and direct the execution of strategic visions, missions, goals, and the objectives to carry them out; (2) maintain current production, quality, cost, and delivery through existing systems (processes and procedures); (3) continuously improve through incremental changes in overall business processes as well as through everyone's individual daily work task processes to achieve set objectives; and (4) make innovative breakthroughs to leap ahead of competition or solve the organization's problems.

Because it is unrealistic to rely completely on breakthroughs, the emphasis must be on the first three requirements, and especially on using *Let's Work Smarter, Not Harder* methods in all areas of your business or organization. Managers must shift their paradigms and become open to implementing new, innovative concepts and new strategies toward continuous process improvement (see Figure 1.1).

In the arena of global competition, adopting an approach of strategic change for continuous improvement and measurement is the only path toward growth. Management simply cannot rely on old traditional strategies

	Traditional quality improvement	Continuous process improvement
Focus	In selected individual operations	In all operations companywide
Process impact	Various unrelated areas	All end results
Results obtained	Takes years to do, highest priority items/ areas only	Rapid improvement in all areas (administration, services, manufacturing)

Figure 1.1. Comparison of quality results.

and improvement methods. Old methods relied on fixing problems, but you do not have to have a problem to improve systems.

In fact, the same improvement methods can be used to improve systems (processes) everywhere. There are, in fact, many commonalties in administration, service, and manufacturing groups, all relating to the reason you are in business—meeting customer needs to make a profit. Common elements include the following:

- Customers being served
- Linkages between customers and suppliers
- Tasks performed to fulfill customer needs
- Definable customer needs
- Processes involving internal and external customers
- Measurable steps when fulfilling customer needs
- Processes being adjusted to meet customer expectations
- Processes that contribute to the businesses' financial bottom line

The same successful techniques used to review, measure, and improve processes in manufacturing can be used in administration and services groups to ensure continuous overall improvement. The goal is *one program for everyone.*

SENIOR MANAGEMENT MUST HAVE ITS PRIORITIES IN THE RIGHT PLACE

Senior managers usually agree that their companies' products must be focused on the customer, but it is not always clear who the customer is. The fact is that *we are all customers and we are all suppliers,* reversing our roles continuously both within and outside of our own departments or functions. Increased understanding of these customer/supplier relationships (linkages) is an important key to productivity improvement and communications (see chapter 3).

Senior managers easily recognize external customers and suppliers—they are the ones who pay or want money for products and services. It may not be so obvious to them, however, that every business and organization under their direction also has many internal customers and suppliers. Equally important, customer needs exist everywhere—in marketing, sales, manufacturing, engineering, purchasing, supply, human resources, order processing, and so on.

A survey by Rath & Strong (*Modern Materials Handling* magazine, November 1993) identified the fact that many firms do not consider customer satisfaction a top priority. More than two-thirds of the top managers of Fortune 500 companies surveyed said that their company's performance is driven more by internal operating results than by external customer satisfaction. These results are not so surprising considering that 80 percent also stated that employee compensation is not directly tied to any defined measure of customer satisfaction. Yet 87 percent of the managers surveyed believed that delivering value to customers is critical to the success of their companies (see Figure 1.2).

DIFFERENCES IN MANAGEMENT FOCUS

By the end of 1991, many Japanese businesses had fairly well abandoned the total quality management (TQM) concept, which can only eliminate defects to a certain percentage, and were moving toward zero defects management to eliminate *all* defects. This occurred just as U.S. businesses

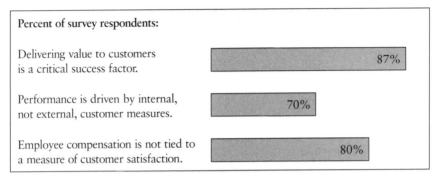

Source: Rath & Strong survey, *Modern Materials Handling* magazine, Nov. 1993. Used with permission.

Figure 1.2. Listening to, but not hearing, the customer.

were implementing TQM on a large scale. Peter Drucker, a leading U.S. management consultant, observed that a company's or organization's goal should be to "prevent defects rather than detect them. You don't need a problem to make things better." Drucker quoted a Toyota official in the *Wall Street Journal* 2 October, 1991 as saying, "we can't use TQM because, at its very best, it can only cut defects to about 10 percent, which on our production rate of 4 million cars would equal 400,000 defective cars and 400,000 dissatisfied customers. This would be unacceptable."

Zero defects sounds like an awesome goal, but it is attainable once a new mind-set is in place. Statistically, many people believe that a zero defects goal is impossible—but if processes are continuously improved, few problems will occur. It does require people to learn problem-solving methods so that each person becomes a system's defect prevention engineer. If you understand why a process (system) is organized as it is, you are better able to make it work, make it work better, or eliminate it altogether. Management must give people the authority to analyze, improve, organize an office or plant layout or an assembly process, get new or proper tools, and obtain necessary education and training. Moving toward zero defects quality means that management must create a strategic vision of zero defects in everyone's mind.

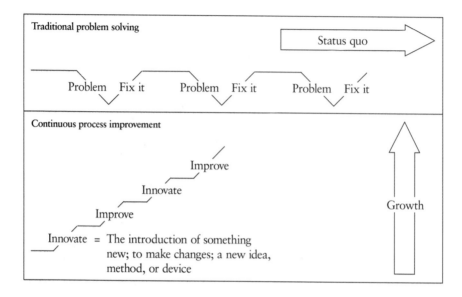

Figure 1.3. Traditional problem solving vs. continuous process improvement.

MANAGEMENT MUST CREATE A CULTURE OF INNOVATION AND IMPROVEMENT

Traditional problem solving usually only succeeds in bringing things back to where they were, instead of improving on and moving beyond the problem. A better approach is to use continuous process improvement methodologies to educate people to focus on improving processes or preventing problems from ever occurring (see Figure 1.3).

What is needed is a return in part to Frederick Taylor's scientific management methodology: rather than relying on engineers to solve all the problems, management must encourage people who are doing the work to take the initiative, study the tasks, and prevent errors.

GOING AROUND IN CIRCLES

When senior managers are not focusing their company on continuous process improvement, it usually gets locked into an endless cycle of feast and famine (see Figure 1.4). This peculiar cycle usually begins with a new

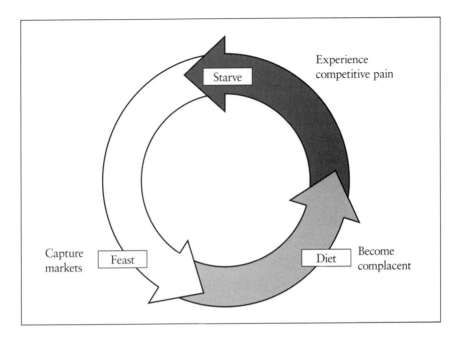

Figure 1.4. Feast-or-famine cycle.

opportunity for a product or service, which is developed, introduced, and aggressively sold to capture new markets. Demand of the new product or service exceeds supply. A growth period follows (feasting). When a business is in this cycle, it experiences growing profits for months, even years. In an attempt to push profits even higher, management may take risks that may jeopardize the business' very existence, by overexpanding its operations in an attempt to avoid the next cycle. Competitive leadership becomes obsessed by the need to improve the bottom line. There's not enough capital, cash flow, space, or energy to do everything. The company's attitude soon becomes, "We have to cut back on something and maintain our high profitability." If the company becomes too complacent (it diets), it conducts little research or process improvement. It stops hiring full-time employees and hires part-timers to dramatically reduce payroll, unemployment insurance, and employee benefit expenses. Profits may increase in the short term, but short-sightedness may result in dramatic losses in the long term. The quality of customer service may drop due to the lack of temporary employees' commitment to customers. Long-term customers may take their business elsewhere. Pressure also comes from competitors that have not gone on a diet but have continued to conduct research and development (R&D) and are constantly improving their processes and services. The supply of the once-new service or product now exceeds demand. The company is now forced to increase spending or look for mergers in an attempt to keep market share (it starves).

When a competitive business is in the starving stage, the desire for the feasting cycle becomes so intense that unbalanced management behaviors have a tendency to increase. Valuable business assets, for example, may be sold at a reduced price to raise capital quickly. Once fear becomes the motivation, chances of short-term benefits overriding long-term benefits is very high. The company may also consider downsizing, which causes low employee morale and a lack of trust in management. Often a company in the starving stage drains its managers' and employees' energy, and the customers, suppliers, and stockholders become dissatisfied. Those caught in this stage of the cycle often become excessed with fear, despair, desire, and/or escape.

Management that drives people to work harder and longer often burns them out until they get sick, quit, or get fired. Once good people start to leave, those remaining are not willing to share ideas for improvement or share job knowledge for fear of jeopardizing their employment. When employees work too much to pick up the work that is now left undone, it stagnates a business and the necessary energy to capture new markets dries up.

Management can avoid this cycle by first changing leadership styles. It must empower learning teams (build quality people and give them process responsibility) to focus strategically on continuous process improvement within daily work processes, and it needs to manage those processes in a cross-functional mode with project management techniques.

WHERE ARE YOU?

With so many successful business leaders today, you'd think there would no longer be a debate regarding the merits of employee empowerment (delegating process responsibility). Some leaders truly are empowering their people; some think they are empowering their people; some wish they were empowering people; and, finally, some leaders dismiss empowerment as rubbish and just a buzzword. Where do you and your leadership efforts stand? Answer yes or no to the following questions.

1. Do you spend more time working on projects than planning and supervising the strategic direction of the department, functional area, or company?

2. Do you feel it is necessary to be involved in everything that is going on in your department, functional area, or company?

3. Do you feel it is necessary to be overly critical with details that aren't highly relevant to your job?

4. Do you spend too much time in the work area(s) performing daily tasks because you enjoy it, even though someone else could do it well enough?

5. Do employees feel that all daily work problems must be brought to your attention?

6. Do you spend too much time doing things for others that they should be doing for themselves?

7. Do you play the role of roving quality assurance inspector to see if employees are doing their jobs correctly?

8. Do you lack confidence and trust in the knowledge, skills, and abilities of employees?

9. Do you ask employees for their ideas and suggestions for resolving problems that arise during their daily work?

10. Do you avoid sharing details, information, and pertinent data with employees for fear it will not be used correctly?

11. Do you often work late hours?

12. Do you work more hours than your staff and employees?

13. Do you have too little time for outside activities, such as family, community activities, hobbies, recreation, and so on?

14. Do you get interrupted frequently by others who request advice or ask you to make a decision for them?

15. Do you have trouble meeting your self-established due dates?

If you answered yes to four or more of these questions, *you may be failing to trust and to delegate responsibility* in a way that effectively empowers (transfers responsibility to) your employees. Review the potential problem areas that may apply.

- *Leadership style:* If you answered yes to

    —Question 1, you may need to pay more attention to strategic long-term planning. Assess your strategies for achieving strategic goals. Establish strategic visions, missions, goals, and objectives, then get out of the way.

    —Question 2, you may be too detail oriented. Excessive attention to details may interfere with your strategic planning and leadership responsibilities. Ask your staff and employees to help you plan, to become involved, and to own an interest (take responsibility) in the department's or company's future.

    —Question 3 and 4, you may need to examine what you like to do versus what your position requires you to do. Perhaps you'd be happier working for someone else. Look for other ways to use your perfection—for example, in forecasting, marketing, customer service, or process flow studies.

- *Development and training of employees:* If you answered yes to

    —Questions 5 and 6, you are probably doing too much of your reports' work. Develop a plan for educating your staff and shifting responsibilities. Establish a knowledge transfer project plan and communicate why you are doing so.

—Questions 7, 8, 9, and 10 relate to trust. Distrust simply becomes a self-fulfilling prophecy. Be careful not to prevent employee development in an unforeseen way. You may be holding back information helpful to performing overall specific tasks.

- *Labor:* If you answered yes to questions 11, 12, and 13, it could indicate you may be understaffed or are not assigning work properly. Examine the work process flow by asking employees to assist you in developing visible work details.

- *Time management:* If you answered yes to questions 14 and 15, it could indicate you may be having time management problems with organizing the usage of your time. Create daily work schedules, then monitor and stick to them. Document and review why deadlines are missed and develop strategies for improving them.

We all need to be reminded from time to time of the major role of management leadership: to get work done through others' efforts, not by ourselves. You know what your actions are.

Empowerment (assuming responsibility) comes when you're willing to let your strategic vision and mission lead. Create a vision of your mission, establish stretch goals, and see what happens. Stretch goals spark new innovative and creative ideas. This is discussed in chapter 6.

DOES YOUR MANAGEMENT STYLE NEED CHANGING?

Implementing a cultural change in any organization is at best difficult. In *The Prince,* Machiavelli first noted more than 465 years ago, "there is nothing more difficult to carry out, nor more doubtful of success, nor more dangerous to handle, than to initiate a new order of things."

Most organizations have a well-defined hierarchy that has been developed and refined over the life of the organization. It is filled with managers trained to operate in rigid, bureaucratic, well-defined functional boundaries and with a vertical chain of command. They perform work in their department and pass it downstream. Many of these departments are not responsible for the end result (product or service) produced, and have little communication with the obvious end customer. Suggested changes for improving business process understanding are discussed in chapter 2.

Senior management must ask middle managers to interact with external customers, to determine their wants and needs, and to incorporate that knowledge into their job functions. This is a vast change for managers who never took the time to learn or keep up with the total process. Can all managers make this transition successfully? Human resource experts Covey (1989), Kouzes and Posner (1987), Senge (1990), and others say success is likely if (1) a beginning point is established that provides a clear and truthful assessment of the current reality; (2) a shared vision of where the organization is headed is articulated; (3) everyone is allowed to feel a part of the organization's purpose; and (4) clear directions, missions, goals, and strategies are formed.

Senior management must carefully consider the skills, education, training, and personal styles of key managers on their staffs. Management style is directly related to personality, which is a function of a person's total life experience. Life experiences may include being highly focused, a risk taker, curious, energetic, a good listener, articulate, a pragmatic dreamer, a purveyor of hope, trustworthy, nonauthoritative, a great public speaker, and a vast traveler. Personalities can be changed, but not easily. *Style* refers to the way managers use their skills, experience, and work background in dealing with peers and employees to achieve desired strategic results.

How do you change a manager's management style? Despite all the written materials available, a lasting and effective personality change at times remains elusive. You can change your management style to one that is compatible with total process management by first understanding what your current management style is. How do you deal with people today? You must thoroughly understand

- What your job requirements are today, and how the established vision, mission, goals, and objectives of the organization affect it

- The quality improvement methods that will be used to implement change
- The needs and skill capabilities of employees reporting to you
- The needs of and what satisfies the customer
- The expected financial results

Second, you must understand what style of management will work best in your job situation. The autocratic style is out today; it's a dinosaur. A country-club atmosphere where little gets accomplished is out as well. You need to be somewhere in between. Last, you must develop a sincere desire for change. You must understand what has been done and what transitions are being implemented; therefore read, study, and learn from others' successes.

Cultural change requires an ability for management to work together across horizontal and vertical boundaries. Dissension and internal conflict must be removed. If management's attitude and behavior does not change, desired culture change will not succeed. This usually means both changing the culture and making structural changes at the same time. Consistent, committed support from senior management is recognized as crucial for successful cultural change. You have probably heard the story of the senior leader who constantly proclaims that "quality is our number-one priority," then demands that something be shipped on time whether it's ready or not. This type of inconsistent behavior will seriously hinder cultural change.

■ ■ ■

In an August 1994 Portland, Oregon, speaking engagement, retired General H. Norman Schwarzkopf (commander of Allied forces during the 1991 Persian Gulf War) talked about his 14 rules to be a leader, the last two of which he said were the most important.

- Rule 13—"When you are in command, take charge."
- Rule 14—"Do what's right."

Schwarzkopf defined leadership as "the ability to get people to willingly do what they normally would not do." He cited four principles.

- Your organization will never get better unless it is willing to admit something is wrong.

- You need to establish goals, and everyone must understand his or her role in achieving them.

- Set standards. When people know what the standards are, they will do a better job than expected.

- Great leaders never tell people how to do their jobs, they establish goals and let ideas flow.

■ ■ ■

PARADIGMS MUST CHANGE

Everyone needs to begin speaking with data that come from documented business systems. Both managers and associates must change their thought patterns from "I think" to "Do we have the data?"—no more "I don't care how you get it done, just get me the results." Management must think about the impacts of system (process) documentation, the discipline required of each associate to follow documented processes, the time necessary to accomplish the tasks, how to improve the skills of all employees, and how to encourage everyone to participate in the process as a learning team member. Typically, process-oriented managers are people-oriented managers (see Table 1.1).

Setting standards for processes is traditionally done by adding the various times it takes each member of a work group to accomplish a given task, finding an average of those times, and dividing the total time by the number of samples. Everyone is expected to adapt to the average. If people can do it in less time, they get rewarded; if they take longer, they get penalized.

A more productive way to set standards is to find out how quickly the fastest person in a group can accomplish a given task, study that person's process steps, then redesign the task so that everyone can do it within that

Table 1.1. Organizational focus vs. process focus.

Organizational focus ⟶	Process focus
Meeting standards	Following procedures
Manage associates	Manage processes
Motivate associates	Remove department bureaucracy
Improve associates	Improve processes
Detect errors	Prevent errors with fail-safe methods
Which associate did it?	Which process allowed this?
Associates can be replaced	Improve associate skills
Know individual job needs	Know my downstream customer and upstream supplier needs
Measure results	Measure processes to improve results
Department focus	Cross-functional process focus
Profit driven	Customer satisfaction driven

same time frame. This sets up a situation where everyone gets rewarded as a team member, not as individuals performing individual processes. Process productivity quickly increases with documented systems and shared procedures.

Continuously simplifying system processes makes everyone successful. Attaining the highest standard possible is better than trying to change people to fit an average standard. When errors occur in processes, you should review and attack process documentation for remedial action rather than discipline the employees who perform the process, because that unnecessarily creates an attitude of fear. Once employees understand that you are improving documentation for their benefit, as well as for that of the organization, they become more inclined to make suggestions and support the error prevention process. Fear must be driven out!

The crux of a process focus is to prevent errors from ever occurring, rather than to detect and correct errors after they occur. It's a prevention versus a detection approach, aimed at zero defects. The best way to handle problems is to prevent them from ever occurring by improving process documentation and implementing fail-safe techniques. The goal is dynamic, fluid, error-free processes throughout all operations.

COMMITMENT TO A NEW WAY

Senior management must be committed to a new way of thinking about improvement. This requires an awareness of the following:

- *Any improvement effort takes time.* Plan for everyone to spend 3 percent to 5 percent of their time working on process improvements. Budget job training at about 5 percent to 15 percent. Focus on three to five key core business processes that can be selected as pilot projects for the entire business. Daily work tasks can be simultaneously reviewed by everyone.

  We suggest that businesses consider their order processing process as a pilot project because it interfaces with more cross-functional activities than other processes within a business. The best midsized to large companies today are completing their total customer order process (the time between finding a customer and collecting accounts receivables) in 45 days or less, while frequently observed times are around 75 days. This can be shortened. Wouldn't you like to be able to do it in 35 days? Just think what you could do with 30 to 40 more days of working capital.

- *Managers and supervisors must create an environment where people feel free to be more self-directed and learn to listen to everyone.* You should stop measuring standard labor hours produced, as this only creates an environment where there is little time for people to work on anything other than output. Most companies with strategic quality improvement plans in place (for example, Motorola, Xerox, Tektronix-Network Display Group) have reserved between 5 percent and 15 percent of an associate's time for the continuous improvement of business and daily work processes.

- *Top management must provide a strategic vision of what the coming cultural change will consist of.* Management's behavior must reflect true commitment—find a process improvement champion

(VP or highest-level group manager) and express a quality-first attitude at all times. Actively manage process reviews and make highly visible rewards a part of your overall improvement process. One of the best examples of a reward that we have seen is acknowledgment of improvement by a senior manager (by the president, a VP, or process champion) in a letter sent to the associate's home.

- *Senior management must "get people on board."* With any organizational change, it's essential that members of the top management group (VPs) convey answers to the following four questions regarding business transformation efforts (whether they are asked or not).

  1. Why is the company changing what it is currently doing?

  2. Why are the new proposals a good thing?

  3. Why do you think employees can execute the transformation (changes) you are proposing?

  4. How is top management going to assist in the proposed transformation (change) efforts?

  You must recognize that if there are any naysayers in the top management group, transformational efforts are doomed (senior management adaptability will provide your biggest challenges). Commitment, communication, and persuasion must be evident at all leadership levels of the business. This requires top managers' (VPs') direct participation; they must commit themselves constantly and sincerely to visible, new strategic directions and measuring transformational progress. The correct measures will pull people toward the overall strategic vision. Senior management participation doesn't prevent you from having problems; it merely helps you deal with them successfully.

- *Provide effective associate empowerment by explaining what it is, why everyone needs to be empowered, and how you will do it.* Management must foster an environment in which people who are taking risks ask themselves, "Would I advise others to invest in this transformation effort? Would I do this with my personal money?"

If you create this type of atmosphere, it will benefit long-term strategic efforts.

- *First-level management needs to educate people in problem-solving techniques* using the seven basic quality tools (check sheets, Pareto diagrams, scatter diagrams, histograms, cause-and-effect diagrams, flowcharts, and control charts). It is worth noting that control charts are now being replaced with precontrol methodologies as a preventive maintenance tool.

Make sure that handoffs from one process to the next are accomplished without error. If you improve all process linkages, bottom-line results automatically and quickly improve, whatever the product or service.

First-level management can encourage and promote commitment to cultural change with the use of the five Ps.

- *Provide*—Give people information and the freedom to use it.

- *Patience*—Provide the time and encouragement necessary for improvement efforts to succeed. All employees must understand that real improvement takes time and must be a long-term continuous goal that you continuously strive for collectively.

Whenever you implement change, procedures must be updated immediately so that employees can focus on the change. Expect to encounter difficulty when new processes and procedures are first implemented. Be prepared to deal with them. Management must continually encourage employees to keep trying and reinforce their efforts when they do. Remember that 99 percent of all improvement plans will fail if tried for only a short period of time. Continue a process improvement long enough for it to become visible. Everyone must believe that things will get better and that their suggestions and work efforts will result in defect prevention and improved productivity (see Figure 1.5). Few improvements show their true worth immediately. They often take one or two months to become visible. Make sure associates know that time is required for learning before improvement becomes evident.

Speaking of patience, this reminds me of the daffodils my son and I planted when he was three years old. Together we purchased some bulbs, dug holes, put in some bone meal, and stuck the bulbs in the holes (most with the roots pointing down). Once the bulbs were covered with dirt and watered, my son wanted to immediately see the flowers. I explained to him that the flowers would not be visible until spring. I was confident that when spring arrived and he would see the results of his planting, he would be excited. The same goes for business. Plant the bulbs, and hopefully everything will work; the bone meal, good soil, and good weather work together and—if all goes well—we'll get the pretty results we wished for. All of the bulbs may not grow, but we hope the ones that do grow and bloom will make a big difference. The same is true of suggested process improvements; some will make an instant impact and others will take time (try and try again).

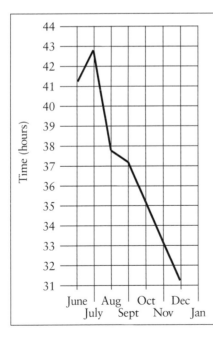

Improvement efforts needs approximately one month to show true gains because

- They demand new procedures
- Difficulties will be encountered
- They take time to learn

99 percent of improvement plans will fail if only tried for a short period of time; plan on a minimum of two months.

Leaders must provide encouragement to keep efforts moving and show gains.

Management must provide support.

Figure 1.5. Time is required for improvement efforts to show gains.

- *Passion*—Show enthusiasm for the improvement of people, processes, and procedures. Continuously display improvement interest and effort, and visually reward results (both positive and negative).

- *Persistence*—Continuously encourage change, improvement, and learning.

- *Publicize*—Provide recognition of change. Encourage everyone to get on the bandwagon. Get people saying "What do I need to do?" or "How can I get involved?"

CONCEPTS OF PROCESS CONTROL

Two basic kinds of control are common in any particular organization: *self-control* and *management control*. Self-control typically involves following established procedures, and management control usually involves the establishment of procedures (systems documentation) as well as the discipline to make sure employees follow them. Inexperienced or new people will usually be working under supervision, with a specific set of instructions on how to do their job. Experienced people, on the other hand, know they can accomplish their tasks with minimal instruction and supervision and often feeling they do not have to follow established procedures. They must, however; there's a constant flow of engineering changes continuously requiring procedure changes and necessitating that everyone follow procedures for error-free production. Problems most often occur when procedures are violated.

With a continuous improvement philosophy in place, procedures will never be static. Experienced or not, employees of all levels must be trained to follow existing procedures and be encouraged to think about continual improvement and simplification of their daily work tasks.

There are two requirements for productive self-control: First, you must receive correct information, data, materials, products, or services from your suppliers; and second, your daily work tasks must be documented and followed. To test the process, document what you are actually doing now and compare it with what you are supposed to be doing. There should be a match. If there is not, your existing procedures are not properly documented. Look for decision and action steps identified in the process. If these are missing, someone else who knows the process more thoroughly will have to be constantly consulted when something goes wrong. Look also for underlines, highlights, added notes, and so on that may indicate process documentation problems. Revise your process documentation until it matches what you do. Reviewing processes is demonstrated in chapter 7.

Defect elimination is very difficult if actual tasks do not match the documented tasks. You must be able to observe what you are supposed to do. With the vast amount of change occurring in most processes today, it is critical that procedure documentation is visibly in place, easy to follow, accurate, and controlled (a requirement of ISO 9000 series and QS-9000 documentation).

Management must encourage people to be ever-vigilant about improving their work processes by helping them focus on changes that will bring about continuous improvement in their daily work. This is discussed in chapter 9. Managers must make sure that process knowledge, changes, and improvements are communicated to everyone, and that everyone is using the same process documentation. There is one process for everyone who performs the same task.

The goal is to get continuous improvement through small-step increments of improvement in your processes. It is always preferable to have a slower improvement or change rate that is under control than a faster improvement rate that is out of control. Technological breakthroughs are nice, but most improvement is achieved in small, incremental steps. Management must make continuous improvement an ongoing process and part of everyone's job description.

Good management means establishing control, which we believe means maintaining and continuously improving all functional work procedures. Like continuous improvement, procedure improvement should also be an item in everyone's job description if productivity improvement is your company's ultimate goal. Management must provide the resources to develop and maintain standard procedures and methods to spread process knowledge among all team members.

In most administration and service areas of companies we have visited, standard procedures are usually lacking or out of date. Senior management must show an interest in what people are doing by walking up to anyone in the company and having a conversation involving these questions.

1. Do standard procedures exist for this process?

2. Are they accessible? Do people know where to find them?

3. Do people follow the standard procedures? *Are they visible?*

4. Are they enforced by everyone?

5. Is there adequate training for existing procedures?

6. Can the procedures be made mistake-proof (fail-safe)?

DID YOU FIND WHAT WE FOUND?

Work is often viewed in administration and services as an event, not a process. When an attempt is made to correct problems, the person who made the mistake is simply asked "What did you do?" or "What happened?" This forces them to recall the situation as it was months ago. But in most cases, people will not remember all the details. Without documented procedures, methods simply evolve over time and are verbally handed down from one person to another, often with no rationale as to why they are still being used.

An example we discovered in one particular office was hilarious. It was policy that whenever this group processed 100 pieces of similar hard-copy documentation, it had to be rubber-banded before sending it to the next department. A new person asked, "What's this rubber band for?" After asking almost everybody in the office, one of the older, senior employees said, "It started 35 years ago; we used to band the documents together so they wouldn't blow apart while taking them from one building to another!" Handed down over time, the task now simply wasted time and energy. It had evolved into batch processing with little process flow.

When we examine daily task functions in many companies and organizations, we find that most procedures are only in people's minds—thus invisible to other workers as well as management. If processes are not visible or documented, they cannot be properly shared, followed, or analyzed for improvement.

Often processes are viewed as events, and employees can be wrongly measured on the work they perform. Measuring for improved performance is nearly impossible without documented procedures. Employees should be measured on how well they perform documented processes and if they do them right the first time.

Most processes have more similarities than differences. A unifying element of all processes is that each and every person working within the process has a customer for whatever he or she is doing. Everything we do has a process connected with it. All processes can be documented, and most (up to 87 percent of them) can be standardized.

THERE ARE DIFFERENT DESIGN STEPS

Management leadership must understand that administration, services, and manufacturing all use processes to produce their end result, but designing or creating the initial process each of them uses is quite different.

When designing processes for administration and services areas, you

- Identify the work you do with a process map.

- Identify who your customers are for your end result.

- Identify what you need from your suppliers.

- Flow together all of the preceding activities.

- Identify non–value-adding activities, remove delays, and establish daily work procedures to be followed.

- Establish improvement goals and throughput time measures.

When designing processes for manufacturing areas, you

- Identify external functional requirements for the product.

- Determine the characteristics critical for each of the fundamental requirements.

- Determine how to control each characteristic: by part, by process, or by both.

- Determine the specifications of each characteristic.

- Determine the process capability of each characteristic. If the capability index is less than 2, redesign the product or process or select different materials as required.

- Establish daily work procedures to be followed during manufacturing.

Notice that the two process design steps are quite different. Once a manufacturing process is designed and its procedures documented, the same process steps used in the administrative and services areas can be used to analyze and improve manufacturing process flows.

MANAGEMENT MUST FOCUS ON ELIMINATING PROCESS VARIATION

Process variation is too often the rule rather than the exception, siphoning off employee energy that could be converted into increased productivity. All variation has a cause, although many of the causes lie dormant and undiscovered. Uncovering them can be done easily by using the seven traditional quality tools: check sheets, Pareto diagrams, scatter diagrams, histograms, cause-and-effect diagrams, flowcharts, and control charts.

Unfortunately, these tools are most typically used in a detection mode (find-and-fix) when they should be used in a prevention mode. Using quality tools to prevent problems enables you to not only prevent mistakes, but to continually improve processes. To ensure a reduction in defect rates, have your quality assurance personnel review process procedures, not end products or services.

■ ■ ■

In the average business, 20 percent of the company's resources are used to find, correct, and prevent errors in processes. Donald Blem, vice president of operations at Advanced Technology Laboratories (Bothell, Washington) and at the time a Tektronix business unit manager was quoted in *Modern Materials Handling* magazine (1987) that by improving processes, the following occurred in his business unit.

- 25 percent reduction in assets required
- 25 percent reduction in personnel
- 40 percent reduction in factory space
- 82 percent reduction in inventory
- 30 percent reduction in scrap and rework
- 50 percent increase in labor efficiency
- 85 percent reduction in throughput times
- 77 percent reduction in setup times

■ ■ ■

SPEND TIME WITH PROCESSES

When management starts to work with processes, it must let long-term thinking override short-term needs. This means you must think in terms of total business processes, along with the individual process functions, groups of events, or departments (silos). Senior management must strategically lead this effort; in fact, the effort must be directed from the top or it will not be effective. Senior management must establish cross-functional teams and "walk the talk"—get out of the office and talk to other departments and employees. A U.S. Government Accounting Office (1991) study of 20 selected companies could not stress enough the importance of top management leaders demonstrating, not simply talking about, a commitment to process management through their daily actions. If a number could be set on the amount of time senior management directly spent on quality-related activities in these companies it would probably be about 20 percent. Without quick action on changes required, efforts will usually get bogged down. Companies can no longer afford a disconnected process management approach where individual groups focus only on their own activities. It takes an overall approach to eliminate the many problems and non–value-adding items that are being passed from group to group and process to process.

DRIVING IMPROVEMENT

The traditional control cycle at the heart of TQM is the plan-do-check-act (PDCA) cycle shown in Figure 1.6. Originally proposed by Walter Shewhart and W. Edwards Deming in 1946, this cycle is still fundamental to most quality activities today. Well-proven over the years, the PDCA cycle provides the means for companies to set goals and create plans, implement the plans, check results, and act on and incorporate the results into the next planning stage. It is a rigorous approach to problem elimination.

The improvement cycle consists of four tasks in the planning quadrant, six in the doing quadrant, four in the checking quadrant, and four in the actions quadrant. The PDCA cycle provides a structured approach to eliminating waste. Hoshin methodology (discussed in chapter 6) begins the PDCA cycle at the check stage. If you know that things need to be improved and you admit that things could be better, it is necessary to begin by first checking or measuring to see where you are today. Begin your improvement efforts by gathering facts and process data. As discussed earlier, effective problem solving begins by establishing what the current situation is so that you can determine where you want to be. Use process and results criteria to measure where you are, then act: Establish what actions you will take to make the necessary process or operational changes. When these are defined, plan: Establish plans for long-term and short-term goals to eliminate waste. Then do: Implement the plans; you are now back at the checking stage. This modification of the PDCA cycle is best for ongoing strategic projects or activities.

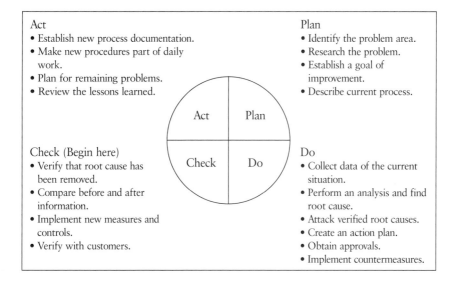

Act	Plan
• Establish new process documentation.	• Identify the problem area.
• Make new procedures part of daily work.	• Research the problem.
• Plan for remaining problems.	• Establish a goal of improvement.
• Review the lessons learned.	• Describe current process.
Check (Begin here)	**Do**
• Verify that root cause has been removed.	• Collect data of the current situation.
• Compare before and after information.	• Perform an analysis and find root cause.
• Implement new measures and controls.	• Attack verified root causes.
• Verify with customers.	• Create an action plan.
	• Obtain approvals.
	• Implement countermeasures.

Figure 1.6. Traditional PDCA control cycle.

■ ■ ■

At a dinner meeting in 1991, Shigeo Shingo, the father of Toyota's production system, suggested that do and check could be combined into what he called, *self-check:* "Did you arrive at the goals you established? If not, continue the cycle, establishing new actions to take to meet the goals."

■ ■ ■

Each part of the check-act-plan-do (CAPD) control cycle requires that you take specific actions and use appropriate tools when establishing process goals (see Figure 1.7).

• In the checking stage, verify that root causes have been removed and compare before and after process information with the established goals. Verify through customer feedback and financial results

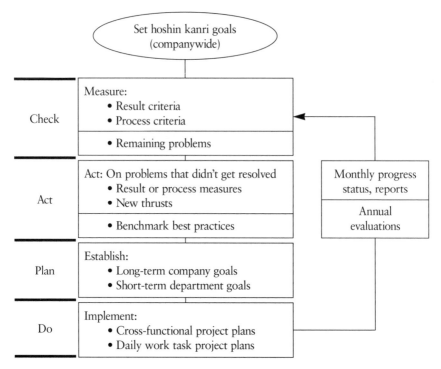

©1993 Caravatta & Associates.

Figure 1.7. CAPD cycle with hoshin planning.

that requirements have been met. Implement new measures and controls if necessary. Use histograms, precontrol charts, graphs, and Pareto charts to measure process results.

• In the actions stage, review the lessons learned whether the outcome was positive or negative. Analyze what went well, what could be improved, and what could be done differently. Develop what actions to take for dealing with any remaining problems and establish plans for further actions. Establish new process documentation if necessary and enforce that it be followed. The tools used are process documentation, training in new procedures, continuous CAPD cycle, and customer feedback.

- In the planning stage, identify strategic areas to be addressed. Research the areas/problems with internal and external customers. Establish a goal of improvement and review the current process procedure. The tools used are strategic plans, documentation control, process maps, graphs, and control charts. Once a process is well-established, documented, and controlled, it becomes a standard to work from. The cycle then becomes standardize-do-check-act (SDCA). When using SDCA, everything begins with a review of the standard process being used.

- In the do stage, implement the plans. Collect data about the current process. Use check sheets to prioritize and tally how many of each type of problem or occurrence exists. Use a Pareto chart to prioritize data gathered with a check sheet. Use a cause-and-effect diagram to determine if the cause is manpower (labor), method, machine, material, or environment-related. Ask the "five Ws and an H" questions: *who, what, where, when, why,* and *how.* Then create an action plan and verify that root causes have been removed. Perform a cost/benefit analysis to determine if the costs for improvement are within reason. Obtain approval of expenditures to implement the plan and, finally, implement necessary countermeasures.

In order to complete goals or objectives that span several layers of control, there will often be subprojects at other levels. These projects should also be done within their own CAPD cycle so that everyone is using the same process. Setting goals and driving them throughout the company or organization requires that everyone become involved, which improves communications and understanding.

ARRIVING AT THE OPTIMUM

Eastern cultures' senior management is currently implementing a more structured approach to innovation, while the West's senior management is trying to promote more teams with employee empowerment. The patterns of each others' past thinking are still very evident: Eastern includes small incremental steps to change culture, Western includes managing projects. Eastern cultures spend a great deal more effort in establishing a company-wide habit of improvement. Their goal is to improve with a continuous stream of small-step improvements by all those performing daily work. In contrast, the West relies on major programs and problem-solving approaches that focus on projects only or on new technologies that promise big gains. Eastern management ensures that established goals are diffused (deployed) throughout the entire organization through staff coaching. Emphasis is on self-improvement and do-it-yourself improvement at every level of the organization. A sense of process ownership is fostered.

The advantages in Eastern culture include the following: management promotes simplicity by making investments in small, incremental improvements; it has lower risks; steady, consistent improvements are achieved through an integration of everyone's efforts; it builds on everyone's knowledge and skills and their existing experience.

The advantages in Western culture include the following: management promotes major projects that hopefully provide larger gains in a short time frame for business leadership (if gains are not achieved in a short time frame, management often withdraws its support); benchmarked technology trends are easier implemented through major projects.

The disadvantages in Eastern culture include the following: management requires vast preparation and training before implementation; it is hard to implement new benchmarked trends in new technology.

The disadvantages in Western culture include the following: projects can become too complex and require high risk, large investments, and a target time lapse between planning and implementation. Dramatic change usually requires management to make a new structure change.

In both environments, management must remove the undesirable management-by-crisis syndrome.

- Many times management itself is the biggest obstacle to creating a creative and innovative workplace. The traditional habits of overseeing everything, following chains of command, maintaining the same organizational structures, and hoarding information are hard to break. Managers must examine how they may unintentionally be preventing employee participation.

- If you can't change the management, then replace the management. Face the fact that no matter how hard you try or what you do, some managers will simply refuse or be unable to adapt to the new realities resulting from organizational (cultural) change.

- Managers must focus the efforts on breaking down functional and organizational barriers that create customer value and speedy responses. Addressing such issues as learning, change management, organizational self-awareness, and balancing order with chaos will be central to a more holistic approach to increasing customer value. Managers must continuously reinvent themselves.

- Managers must understand that the organization's measurement system strongly affects the behavior of employees. What you measure (customer satisfaction, internal processes, innovation, and improvement activities) should drive financial performance.

- Management's key responsibility must be to ensure that business systems are documented, made defect-free, and then followed in all environments. Inspection and rework activities must be replaced with fail-safe methods to prevent mistakes from occurring. Then profitability will automatically go up (see Figure 1.8).

The Best of the Best Corporations in Process Management participated in a management colloquium held by Arthur D. Little (Executives Say 1995). They came up with the following list of lessons and recommendations for process managers.

- Top-down, cost-driven approaches to process reengineering have been largely discredited.

- Most lasting results are obtained when initiatives are started by middle managers who deliver results that get senior management's attention.

Quality technique	Cost	Impact
Fail-safe methods	($)	Zero defects No wasted resources
Self-check	($$)	Small delay Fix myself
Successive check	($$$)	Minor delay Send back to fix
Final inspection	($$$ $$$)	Major delay Send back to fix Reschedule work Additional inspection
Field failure (defect reaches customer)	($$$$$ $$$$$)	Customer dissatisfaction Loss of market share Warranty costs Administrative costs Inventory handling Shipping costs

Figure 1.8. Economic impact of defects.

- Employees will be uncomfortable about fuzzy change and think of organic management tools as more tacit, internal, and intuitive than other current approaches.

- Look for and capitalize on unconscious competencies or values that persist across market cycles and leadership changes.

- Look at the boundaries of each process.

- Focus on people.

CHAPTER 2

CROSS-FUNCTIONAL BUSINESS RELATIONSHIPS

AIM OF THIS CHAPTER

The overall goal of improving processes is to lower the breakeven point of what it costs to do business. To do this, everyone must be thinking about defect prevention and throughput time (process velocity) in their business and daily work processes. Care must be taken that changes are not just implemented for changes' sake. Improving cross-functional business processes does no good if it costs more than customers are willing to pay for the change. There needs to be an overall strategy in place to ensure that the changes will be fully integrated with all other downstream processes. You must keep in mind that to remain competitive all process activities may no longer reside within one business or one country (consider a virtual organization such as NIKE). The costs of the entire process are what customers pay for, and those costs determine whether a product or service is competitive.

This strategy must be managed cross-functionally and include all downstream processes, associates, suppliers, and customers. Bring people together that participate in a total process, and merge the thinking and actions of functional groups for joint performance. The leap-frogging

improvements that occur will come about via the many horizontal organizational structures that exist in companies and organizations, but are
seldom defined or properly managed as one. A large part of the costs
incurred are between activities. Major change opportunities exist within
this framework.

You must get away from running a rigid hierarchy, which is counter
to being innovative and adaptive to change. You have an opportunity to
build bridges to connect your various functions and departments.

■ ■ ■

The following translation is paraphrased from a 1986 article in the
Japanese magazine *Voice*. Hajime Karatsu, a Japanese quality control
expert, said that he and many of his colleagues were saddened to see
one American industry after another go under due to poor assembly line
practices. Karatsu believed that the crux of the problem was the failure by
U.S. industry to organize workers to function cooperatively in an overall
process.

No longer was it enough to just do your own job properly; each
worker had to be responsible for the whole product. Karatsu said that collective responsibility is just common sense. The old concept of time and
motion studies and rigid division of tasks (scientific management, pio-
neered by Frederick W. Taylor) was wrong. Taylor's logic suggested that if
employees' duties were carefully analyzed and allocated, the total process
should function with maximum efficiency. But people are not machines,
and the theory ultimately did not hold up.

Japanese-style managers revived the old sense of craftsmanship,
which they believe brings a well-spring of enthusiasm and pride to one's
work. Craftsmanship is possible only when employees have some leeway
in a task—a chance for personal input. Karatsu also stated that the simpler an idea (removing steps, parts used, and so on), the more important
it is that all elements function properly.

■ ■ ■

VERTICAL VS. HORIZONTAL ORGANIZATIONS

When I visit companies to talk about process improvement, I often ask how work gets accomplished. The host inevitably begins by showing a vertical company organization chart. Vertical organization charts typically show lines of reporting authority; this is their intended purpose. They are quickly understood by managers everywhere, because they show at a glance who works for whom and who has responsibility for what. I then like to ask the person whose name is in the top box what he or she does. The usual response is that he or she manages all the functions in the boxes below. This we know is not true; that's what the managers of those departments do (typically the top thinks and the bottom responds). What the vertical organization chart does not indicate is how work actually gets done. Nor does it set the stage to encourage the right process behaviors. The vertical organization neither accommodates changing flows nor provides a culture that can take advantage of today's process knowledge. This requires a map that diagrams process work flows and their interrelationships. If overlaid on a vertical organization chart, these processes would typically be oriented horizontally.

The organization chart in Figure 2.1 shows the gray areas where the important work interrelationships, communications, linkages, and handoffs between functions or departments occur. These are what the person in the top box of the organization chart should focus on and manage. Processes almost always cut across the vertical organization structure and often include other OEM businesses or countries. When function managers focus only on their function, they do not see how activities directly interrelate. Try adding together the opportunities for error prevention in a

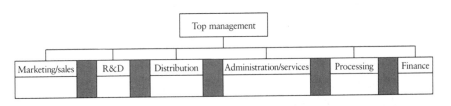

Figure 2.1. Traditional vertical business organization showing gray areas where most process problems occur.

total process; you will be surprised at how many exist. When senior managers understand this, continuous improvement of business and daily work processes becomes possible. Horizontal structures must be flexible, focused on quality, and value creating—which means that no two structures will ever be mapped exactly alike.

In many organizations, work usually gets done regardless of the way a company is organized, but with hidden inefficiencies. "How does the work get accomplished?" is actually a trick question, but we ask it because it so aptly illustrates how companies think about their organizational structure. The real question is, *"What process thinking do you use to accomplish the work?"* Look at Table 2.1 to see if you recognize your business. In many companies we have observed, management does not devote enough time to studying and analyzing how work actually gets done. Until this happens, substantial productivity improvements are impossible.

If you ignore horizontal process management, you reduce the chances to prevent defects, which means your company may not grow and prosper (see Figure 2.2). In relative terms, it doesn't take a lot of money to start working on horizontal processes; it simply takes sweat. (This reminds me of what a teacher once said: "Before the mighty gods invented genius, they invented—how shall I put it—sweat.") The effort requires that you encourage people to start thinking about the processes within which they are working; using brainpower on the processes frees money for other uses.

Table 2.1. Do you recognize your business?

Do You Recognize Your Business?
1. Each department or function in the reporting structure is independently directed, managed, or controlled from the top.
2. Each department or function establishes its own expected end result, based on its own responsibilities, to be achieved by its own staff and subordinates.
3. Each department or function has its own independent budget.
4. Each department or function competes with the others internally for resources.
5. Departments or functions are managed vertically, even though work processes flow horizontally across them.

Vertical management thinking	Horizontal management thinking
Motivate the workforce.	Remove barriers.
Find out who did something wrong.	Find process problem.
Blame a responsible person.	Study the process, remove errors.
Fix everyone's attention on profits.	Fix everyone's attention on process quality.
Measure productivity.	Measure processes: throughput time, defects per unit
Reward individual performance.	Reward team performance.
Establish working orders.	Define/document procedures.

Figure 2.2. Vertical and horizontal management thinking.

HORIZONTAL PROCESS HISTORY

I'll use the activities of a sheep farmer to explain the transformation that occurred in the processing of wool garments. In the 1920s, 1930s, and 1940s, farmers had complete control of the total wool garment process used. Farmers raised sheep and sheared them themselves. After shearing, the wool was stored until the farmer's wife could spin it onto yarn spools. She would then sort the spun spools of wool into similar textures, colors, cleanliness, and so on. Some wools were dyed, and others were left in their natural colors before being made into sweaters, vests, and so on. A finished garment was taken to market by the farmer and bartered or sold to customers. Immediate feedback was received from customers. If they liked what they saw and agreed on a price, they bought the goods. If they didn't, the farmer would take them back home, bringing either good or bad news with him.

He would immediately discuss and correct problems. A problem could have occurred anywhere in the process: how the sheep were fed and cared for; how the wool was sheared, spun, sorted, stored, dyed, and made into garments; or the price offered for sale or barter. The farmer had total understanding and control of each process step. A problem was effortlessly identified and removed.

With the arrival of the industrial revolution, the processing of wool garments changed dramatically. Each step in the sheep farmer's process became a specialty process. The farmer raised the sheep. The wool was sheared by professional shearers. The wool was purchased by wool traders, then sold to various weavers. The weavers dyed and wove patterned or colored cloth that was sold to clothing manufacturers. The clothing manufacturers designed, manufactured, and sold the garments to retail outlets. The retail outlets sold the garments to customers. Where in this chain of events did the feedback go if a customer was dissatisfied with a purchased garment? I'm sure you know the answer. The workers in each activity were responsible for their own quality output. A backward chain reaction started, with each trying to blame the other for what occurred. After trying several times to find a guilty party, each process step (owner) established an outgoing inspection process. All process steps also began inspecting incoming goods with a similar activity, making sure that only good items were received. Each handler along the way added a non–value-adding cost to all future purchases of wool garments. Many product and service providers today still use similar specialty, costly methods.

BACK TO BASICS: RETURN TO AN UNDERSTANDING OF TOTAL PROCESS MANAGEMENT

When starting to work with processes, long-term thinking must override short-term needs. This means you must think in terms of total business processes, along with the individual process functions, groups of events, or departments (silos). Senior management should lead this effort; in fact, the effort must be directed from the top or it will not be effective. Senior managers must establish cross-functional teams and walk the talk—get out of their offices and talk to other OEM providers, departments, and employees. A U.S. Government Accounting Office study of 20 selected companies could not stress enough the importance of top management leaders demonstrating—not simply talking about—a commitment to quality through their daily actions (GAO 1991). If a number could be set on the amount of time senior management directly spent on quality-related activities in these companies, it would probably be about 20 percent.

Companies can no longer afford a disconnected approach where individual groups focus only on their own activities. The ability to break down the internal organizational barriers that block the view to future processes is a must. Collaboration between groups is no longer optional. It takes an overall approach to eliminate the many errors and non–value-adding items that are passed from group to group and process to process.

——————————————— ■ ■ ■ ———————————————

Joe Guglielmi, a 30-year veteran of IBM and now head of Taligent (a joint venture between IBM and Apple to develop an object-oriented operating system to compete with Microsoft and Next, which was acquired by Apple in 1997 as part of its improvement strategy), is a believer that empowerment without process leads to anarchy. He talks about hands-on management: "If you never experience the problem but only read about it you are so detached, it is hard to imagine coming up with the solution."

Guglielmi likes to measure performance, which requires some discipline. He asks questions like, "What's your process for doing this?" or "How do you know you can repeat it?" This approach meets resistance from highly creative types—but when they try it and if it works, they love it. Guglielmi had Big Blue's bulky procedures manual entombed in plastic in the middle of Taligent's plant floor; they didn't want anyone using it. When asked why he did this, he said, "They were too confining, weren't written for the workers, and they're useless."

——————————————— ■ ■ ■ ———————————————

We advocate steering away from the program-of-the-month situation that is prevalent in many businesses. While valuable in specific instances, most don't address error prevention but only seek one "splash" of success, and simply end up using people's energies in an uncoordinated way.

Joel Barker often states that "many companies are blinded by their past successes, which guarantee little in today's changing global marketplace." W. Edwards Deming often said, "If you always think what you always thought, you'll always get what you always got." I once heard him say it at a seminar in Los Angeles. Progress is impossible if you always do things the way you've always done them. And the only way to change things for the long term is to continuously review your cross-functional business and daily work processes and adapt them to the continuously changing environment of revised customer needs—cost, quality, variety, and response.

TOTAL BUSINESS PROCESSES AND THEIR IMPACT ON TTT

Work gets done through processes, and processes should drive the way your business or organization is structured. Vertical structures are basically reporting systems that provide no real insight to how the actual work gets done. They don't show links or connecting functions. Most activities in any business or organization take place in all directions, but should all be considered direct handoffs to downstream customers. There are many inputs, many processes, and many outputs (see Figure 2.3), all of which have a direct impact on total throughput time (TTT). Review how external inputs, the internal business functions, and external outputs relate to each other in real life. Only major handoffs are identified; many more arrows could be added to depict the average organization. They were left off the example for clarity.

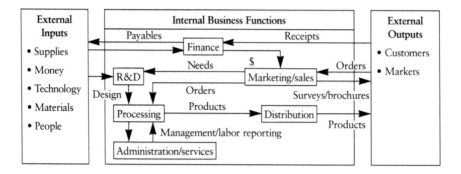

Figure 2.3. Cross-functional working relationships in businesses and organizations.

■ ■ ■

External inputs:
- New technologies, processes
- Outside supplies
- Money to operate the business with the best people
- Available materials—no problems with delivery
- People's new skills

Internal business functions:
- Flow, handoffs
- Reduced expenses

External outputs:
- Market niches
- Customer needs
  - —Quality: the best
  - —Cost: the lowest
  - —Flexibility: produce things the way I want them
  - —Response time: shortest, quickest delivery time

■ ■ ■

ACTIVITY SILOS

Activities traditionally take place within a business or organization in silos—separate functions, departments, or groups working independently of each other, each group trying to please its perceived customer, the "top" or manager. Isolated silo activities often preclude management from being aware of the needs of other internal activities, as well as all-important external customer needs. All reporting areas think they are doing a good job, but no one is making sure that all linkages to all downstream customer requirements are met—and usually they are not. Frequently there are few documented horizontal processes in place between individually, separately managed groups.

H. James Harrington's book, *Business Process Improvement* (© 1991, reproduced with permission of the McGraw-Hill Companies), lists a startling fact—40 percent to 70 percent of white collar effort in typical administration and internal service functions adds no value to products or services (p. 17). And this applies to all major departments within these functions—sales, marketing, engineering, order processing, finance, and so on. By setting up structured horizontal processes between these silo groups, handoff errors and the bureaucracy that exists between them can be greatly reduced, resulting in overhead cost savings of up to 50 percent. Overhead typically represents up to an astounding 80 percent of the costs in administration and internal service groups and development engineering organizations, and up to 50 percent in manufacturing. Every company has an opportunity to cut overhead costs in half if it has not yet implemented cross-functional process management. Failure to address total cross-functional processes can also result in a company's heading in the wrong direction strategically. Resources may be poured into the wrong functions, internal group competition may increase, and people's energies may be diverted from value-adding tasks. It's hard for one group to solve a problem in another group; the problem can be solved only when decision makers work together for the good of the total process.

CUSTOMER ORDER PROCESSING EXAMPLE

This silo function is common to most companies and provides a good example of a total process with many activities that must take place in a horizontal direction (see Figure 2.4). To quickly analyze the efficiency of your order processing function, or any other overall business function, ask two fundamental questions.

1. Can everyone work through all the related activities within the process in a short enough time to be responsive to the end customer?

2. Is the cost in line with all the activities necessary to complete the process and with the end price to the customer?

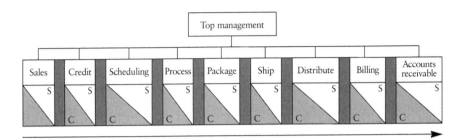

Figure 2.4. Customer order processing is a horizontal activity.

A typical scenario for order processing is as follows. The task usually begins with sales supplying all the information used downstream in the processes: production requirements, deliveries, credit data, and so on. This information generally directs the production process; the more complicated the end product or service, the more complicated the coordination process becomes across the organization. The more coordination that is required, the greater the chance to negatively affect the customer. If sales doesn't provide the right information to scheduling, for example, the downstream processing function can't proceed. Likewise, if information is not correct on the sales order or is delayed, packaging will not be able to include the correct items in the box. Incorrect addresses will affect shipping, distribution, and billing. Often the billing process has been set up to serve the internal department, not the customer. Any problems with customer order billing provides a convenient "tool" for customers to avoid payment, which lengthens total throughput time and affects the bottom line. As shown in Figure 2.5, there are many internal downstream customers in the customer order processing function. This is a good place to start a process review in most companies, since it requires participation from each interfacing area.

Every time an order is handled, a customer is handled. Following an order through its process enables a company to identify gaps or shortcomings, areas where an order can "fall through the cracks." It also identifies where costs can be cut, time can be saved, and technology can be

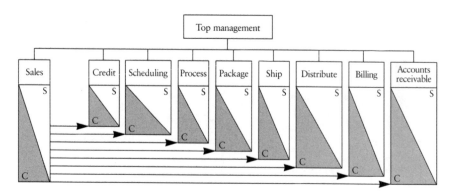

Figure 2.5. View of all true downstream customers.

effectively applied. By mapping you will actually allow/enable your associates to look at your company through the customers' eyes. That's a very valuable experience for the associates as well as for the company.

You will find that most areas in need of attention are not in the individual departments, but at the handoffs or junctions where information or accountability change. Whenever you improve your processes to increase efficiency, you will also improve operations, avoid internal competition, and open the potential for increased profits.

Modify the way you do business by understanding what your customers want and ensuring that their needs don't turn into dissatisfiers. When a company's systems (processes) work efficiently, they are focused on satisfying all customer needs (internally and externally), and targeted goals will be achieved that improve financial performance. By studying your processes, you will learn where to fix both obvious and anticipated problems. It takes hard work to improve systems processes, and in most cases it requires a change in process management style (the soft stuff— such as personalities and their interactions—is the hardest to manage).

Many important issues emerge when you begin focusing on your total processes. Group functions become more aligned with each other, a commonality of direction or synergy emerges, and the individuals within the groups become more harmonious. And if you do this as a cross-functional project team, negatives like bureaucratic finger-pointing and assigning blame quickly evaporate. A trust develops among associates who are working toward a common shared vision (goals) or understanding. The quality of communications increases, and the capability and productivity of the total process improves quickly.

Systems thinking is a fundamental element of learning organizations. If problems occur, review the total systems integrated process. The cure lies in understanding interrelationships among your downstream customers and upstream suppliers. Systems thinking is an efficient way to deal with process problems. Process problems are not cheap; you pay someone to make them, then you pay someone to fix them. Once linked functions (cross-functional team members) observe that they can no longer blame one another for slowing down the process due to defects being produced, they have no recourse but to blame the system that produced the end result. As Walt Kelly's character Pogo used to say, "We have met the enemy, and he is us!" Success is influenced through systems disciplines disclosing complex situations in a specific core (business) process. In order for one function to succeed in an integrated systems process, others must also succeed.

Psychologically, organizations will have to get used to dynamic, integrated, shared control: it will be top down, bottom up, and side to side (group process management). There must be a fundamental shift in how we understand and manage business. It's critical throughout a redesign process to evaluate whether change is being made for well-documented business reasons (removing waste) or whether politics, culture, or the organization's current vertical structure are clouding judgment and encouraging only easy changes that aren't necessarily the best decisions.

Caution: Change doesn't come only from research efforts, but from having an organization in which management listens to employees who actually make or market the product or service—employees who hear what customers say. There's no quick fix; establishing a process orientation typically entails a flattening of the vertical reporting hierarchy, comprehensive communications, new systems, and new management responsibilities. Don't fall into the norm of meeting any new situation with meaningless reorganizing. Reorganizing is a wonderful method for creating the illusion of progress. If new structures do not regard cross-functional needs and capabilities of the organization, your business may face severe limitations in its continued success. Build shared visions, missions, goals, and objectives to establish alignment (all functions in a total process heading together in the same direction) before modifying the way you do business to improve customer satisfaction.

CHAPTER 3

CUSTOMER/SUPPLIER RELATIONSHIPS

AIM OF THIS CHAPTER

In this chapter I discuss improvement as it relates to internal and external customers and suppliers. Improvement must always be focused and aimed at the needs of the consumer. Saying this, the consumer must be the most important part of a production or service organization. *You cannot afford to dissatisfy a single customer with your end result product or service.*

You do not have to wait for a crisis to begin improving customer satisfaction. It is good to remember that the Chinese word for *crisis* means both peril and opportunity. Opportunity can arise from what is otherwise thought to be a negative response. Often negative results are starting points for new and better opportunities; consider them treasures. Looked at in this way, negative results can spell brighter prospects instead of failure.

Understanding the definitions of *customers* and *suppliers* is vitally important. It is hard to improve process relationships without this understanding. Internal product specifications all too often do not relate to customers' needs. Furthermore, all customer needs cannot be expressed in terms of quantifiable specifications. For example, "feel" is difficult to quantify. We know that getting close to customers is key to building a successful business in today's service environment. We've learned that it costs five times as much to attract a new customer as it does to retain one you already have. The idea of customer retention is at the heart of building and maintaining a successful business. The key is to bring customers back over and over again by exceeding their needs and expectations—delight them.

DISCIPLINE PRODUCES DEFECT-FREE PRODUCTS

When purchasing goods or services, most of us look for the best quality item at the lowest price. For example, studies show that more than half the population in the United States will buy Pacific Rim products such as TVs, cars, and so on because the products are higher quality (that is, are more defect-free) than their U.S. counterparts. Based on purchasing habit interviews, most people say they expect defect-free products. Understanding customer/supplier relationships in cross-functional business processes improves the probability of producing defect-free products and services. This ingrained process discipline in many Asian businesses enables them to produce defect-free products or services, as opposed to many U.S. business practices that tolerate an acceptable level of defective product.

There are many hidden advantages to producing a defect-free product: faster throughput time, greater quantities, on-time delivery, built-in quality, reduced failure rates, less warranty claims, and better market capture. Defect-free products are the result of improving process quality, which produces a chain reaction of benefits for your business or organization (see Figure 3.1).

Engrave the following chain reaction in your organization: If you improve process relationships, quality and productivity will both improve. When productivity improves, there will be less rework and wasted effort. Costs will decrease because of less inspection and rework, fewer mistakes, fewer delays, and better use of resources. If you can offer products or services at a cheaper cost than your competitors, market share will grow. You will capture the market with better quality and a lower price; finally, this will provide long-term business stability and more jobs.

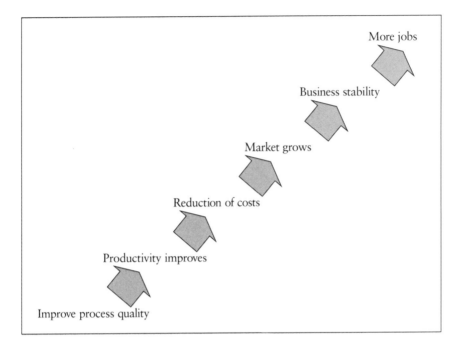

Figure 3.1. Improving process relationships results in a chain reaction of other improvements.

THE CONSUMER IS THE MOST IMPORTANT PART OF A PRODUCT OR SERVICE

During a 1992 National Technological University presentation entitled "Kaizen: An American Approach," William F. Fletcher said that for every customer who complains, there may be up to 24 dissatisfied customers who do not complain. Those dissatisfied customers, however, may tell 10 to 20 people, meaning that 25 dissatisfied customers may influence 250 to 500 potential customers. This is a potential loss of 500 customers, and you may have heard only one complaint!

Based on these data, can your company afford to lose even one customer? We don't believe you can. You must provide products and services that have the highest quality and reliability and meet the most demanding customer needs. To keep bringing your customers back, it will take everything you read, see, hear, and experience. You must prospect for valuable customer information constantly; learning about your customers' requirements is a never-ending task.

Good ideas come from everywhere. If you're not looking for them, you won't recognize them. It's easy to pay so much attention to what you're doing internally that you lose sight of what you absolutely must do to satisfy the basic needs of the purchasing customer. A continuous improvement process focus with conformance to customer requirements aims at this goal through gradual, unending improvements—do it better, make it better, improve things even if they are not broken. Question the three Rs of your supplier services.

- *Responsiveness*—Does each step of each process improve the response to customers?

- *Results*—Does each step improve end results, such as product or service quality or profits?

- *Resources*—Does each step improve the effectiveness of resources such as people and inventory?

UNDERSTANDING THE SUPPLY CHAIN

All work is a series of internal and external customer/supplier links (relationships). These linkages (flows) may not always occur in straight lines—they could be circular, in parallel, or even back-and-forth—but the relationship of events still exist.

As shown in Figure 3.2, a person receives an item from an upstream process supplier (black arrows), adds value through a work process, and passes it on to the next person. If this process is to work smoothly and efficiently, there is an obvious need for understanding all along the supply chain. This can occur only through feedback (white arrows), where the others' needs are considered. These needs can be expressed verbally or graphically and can be documented so that problems can be properly addressed and permanently eliminated. Process documentation is essential if process problems are to be solved and processes improved so that the end result (product/service) will be defect-free.

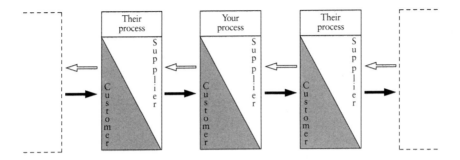

Figure 3.2. Customer/supplier needs model.

■ ■ ■

Thinking of yourself in terms of customer and supplier is usually easy to teach. While working next to a group of financial planners and listening to their phones ring constantly, we showed them how to document their office processes in order to analyze the problem (constant phone interruptions). Once they realized that most of the calls were from suppliers with different expectations as to the information they were providing, the planners (as customers) eliminated what they determined to be a gray area and told their suppliers in what format they wanted information to be sent. Within a month, the unnecessary phone calls were reduced to a minimum, the planners understood that feedback and communications with their suppliers was very important, and the suppliers understood that the planners were their customers and that they needed to meet the planners' needs.

■ ■ ■

All associates must understand that within the company they are both customers *and* suppliers, whether they are designing, selling, accounting, providing or receiving information, or responding to requests. You are a customer when you *receive* and a supplier when you *provide*. Understanding this drives costs down and quality up, because it pushes problems back to where they originated upstream in the process and can be better solved. Think of customer/supplier relationships like tossing a ball back and forth. If the ball is tossed too fast or too hard, you might drop it, fumble it, and have to pick it up again. Learning to toss it just right (defect-free) so that it can be caught easily will result in a good interface between customers and suppliers. Providing something (tossing the ball) and receiving something (catching the ball) occurs on a regular basis in all customer/supplier relationships (communications).

UNDERSTANDING NEEDS

Every function, department, and group within a company or organization exists to fulfill customer needs, whether those of the ultimate and obvious end customer or an intermediate or internal customer. All customers have needs that are strikingly similar, no matter who they are: getting personal attention (everyone likes to feel individually important); receiving a product or service that is of high quality, low cost, and provided as wanted (meets or exceeds customer needs); and being served in the shortest possible time (prompt delivery).

WHAT KIND OF SATISFACTION ARE YOU PROVIDING?

Companies satisfy customers in different ways and at different costs (see Figure 3.3). The levels of customer satisfaction diagram shows four scenarios in which most suppliers satisfy their customers and the costs involved in doing so.

The upper left quadrant is the ideal and delights customers; the lower left quadrant should be avoided. Look to see where you and your company are, and create a focus on where you want to be in the future. The majority of companies satisfy their customers with activities in the upper right quadrant: providing high quality at a relatively high cost. Departments are managed as independent functions, and there is a lack of process documentation throughout. Inspection and rework stations are built into the process flow. Every time I ask managers and associates

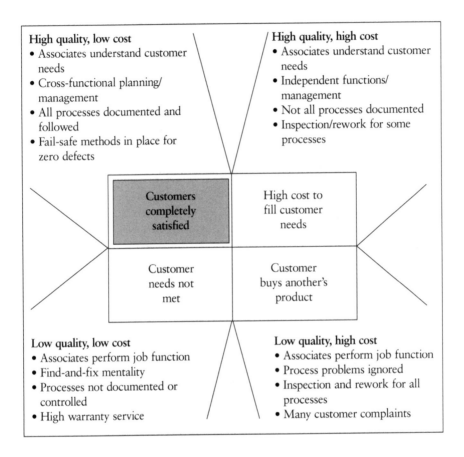

Figure 3.3. Levels of customer satisfaction and their quality/costs.

what kind of quality items their departments or functions are producing, the answer is almost always, "high quality," yet most are observed inspecting quality into the end result. To find out how you measure up, evaluate your performance as a supplier/provider (see Figure 3.4), then as a customer/receiver by answering the questions in Figure 3.5.

High quality and customer satisfaction will flow from understanding and meeting customer needs. The best way to achieve understanding is to

1. Perform a customer satisfaction survey with your customers to identify strengths, weaknesses, and opportunities for improvement.

Evaluate Your Performance as a Supplier

Go through this list of questions with each of your customers. Circle yes or no for each question. Each time you circle a no indicates an opportunity for you to improve your process as a supplier.

1. Do you listen to your customers?... Yes   No

2. Do you communicate with your customers to clarify their expectations? .... Yes   No

3. Do you know how internal customers use your product or service? .... Yes   No

4. Do you know how external customers use your product or service? .... Yes   No

5. Do you deliver products or services designed for customers' ease of use? .... Yes   No

6. Are products or services designed for customers' ease of use?......... Yes   No

7. Do you strive for continuous improvement in everything you do?..... Yes   No

8. Do you focus your improvement efforts on specific critical customer requirements that are related to customers' expectations? .... Yes   No

9. Do you quickly respond to customers' requests for information or other needs?.. Yes   No

10. Do you keep your customers informed of form, fit, or function changes? .... Yes   No

11. Do you keep promises that you make to customers? .... Yes   No

---

Figure 3.4. Supplier quiz.

2. Perform an analysis of cross-functional workflow processes.

3. Then begin planning and implementing cross-functional improvement projects.

4. Apply two process measures to your results measures at least on a monthly basis: total throughput time (velocity) and defects per unit produced. (See chapter 8 to understand how to perform measures.)

Data gathered from linked, cross-functional processes will be much more valuable for change and improvement than data from independently

---

Evaluate Your Performance as a Customer

Go through this list of questions with each of your suppliers. Circle yes or no for each question. Each time you circle a no indicates an opportunity for you to improve your process as a customer.

1. Do your suppliers know your expectations or requirements? .... Yes   No

2. Do you specify your needs or expectations in exact terms and give your suppliers the lead time they need? .... Yes   No

3. Do you know what your suppliers need from you in order to better meet your needs? For example, do your internal/external suppliers need a certain amount of lead time? .... Yes   No

4. If something is not received correctly or promptly from your suppliers, do you provide detailed feedback on a regular basis? .... Yes   No

5. Do you require that your suppliers improve over time? .... Yes   No

6. Do you communicate with your suppliers to ensure that their improvements relate to your needs? .... Yes   No

7. Do you inform your suppliers of changes in your needs or requirements? .... Yes   No

---

Figure 3.5. Customer quiz.

managed silo functions that usually compete for the same resources. Superior customer satisfaction can occur only when everyone in a cross-functional process understands all downstream customers' needs and meets them every time.

■ ■ ■

I was asked to review what happened during a four-days-late delivery situation in which the customer had become very upset after being promised a specified delivery date (see Figure 3.6). Looking at the process, I found that three groups were involved: sales, processing, and distribution. All three thought they had provided excellent service. Sales had met the goals for the month, processing said the product was delivered within the normal timeframe, and distribution said everything was delivered

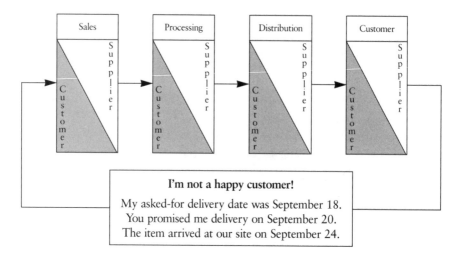

Figure 3.6. Objectives and measurements must be aligned with customers' needs and expectations.

within four days, which was the normal turnaround. Everyone was doing his or her best, but the product was delivered late to the customer.

The culprit turned out to be the sales department's lack of cross-functional process understanding. Sales employees didn't understand the overall downstream processes and promised the customer an unrealistic delivery date. Sales had asked the processing group when the item would be available and were given a specific date it would leave their area. Sales then told the customer that the product would be at their site that same date. They failed to consider the four-day period after the item was produced until distribution had it in the customers' hands. The customer's needs were not met. Sales must be able to explain every nuance of a product or service, or the company and the customer are at risk. This company made a sale, but possibly lost a customer.

Competitiveness demands that you get as close as possible to your customers, both internally and externally. You must adapt to your external customers' demands with internal colleagues from sales, marketing, operations, finance, and so on. Only through systems understanding can you eliminate the problem shown in Figure 3.6. Businesses that fail to grasp the importance of others' requirements and act immediately will fall behind. The critical element, however, goes beyond knowing what must be changed; it's getting the change executed and institutionalized.

One of management's key responsibilities is to ensure that all cross-functional processes are integrated, documented, understood, and followed. Processes must be understood from end to end, all the way to the customer. Inspection and rework cycles must be replaced with fail-safe methods to prevent mistakes from occurring. Goals, objectives, and measurements already in place must be aligned with your customers' needs and expectations. Once integrated processes are flowing error-free, customer satisfaction and profitability automatically go up.

■ ■ ■

INCREASE YOUR BOTTOM-LINE DOLLARS THROUGH INTERNAL CUSTOMER/SUPPLIER RELATIONSHIPS

There is more opportunity to improve your bottom-line dollars with internal process improvement (satisfying internal customer needs) than in trying to increase sales to ultimate customers. You must sell a lot more product to increase sales profits by 10 percent than you would if you improved internal processes by 10 percent. Internal improvements go directly to the bottom line.

Each function, department, group, or organization acts as a supplier when providing an output (information, data, material, product, or service) to all downstream customers. To do this, however, these groups in turn must have their needs fulfilled by all their upstream suppliers. Understanding these organizational, interdepartmental, cross-functional needs leads to everyone's fulfillment and makes the processes work, thus improving productivity. There must be continual interaction and communication between providers and receivers to discuss needs. Everything you do is included in a chain of cross-functional interdepartmental interactions and should be documented and continuously analyzed for improvement. The goal is to not pass problems downstream to someone else; the ultimate goal is zero-defect products and services.

Making incremental, evolutionary, revolutionary change in the organization to meet customer expectations and demands, as well as company needs, is a must. It may require retooling, rethinking processes, reorganizing activities, reinvigorating employees, and rededicating resources. When you constantly exceed the needs and expectations of your customers, *you're doing the right things.* It makes good business sense because it leads to repeat sales.

Everyone must attempt to become better and better at what he or she does by understanding how to use improvement tools to view integrated customer/supplier relationships. To make this an ongoing process, everyone's job description should include a customer satisfaction measurement. Following are four key methods of gathering inputs that will assist you in improving customer satisfaction or documenting the voice of your customer(s).

1. *Customer complaint recording*—It pays to have happy customers. Each and every one of us has customer(s), and we need to measure their satisfaction.

2. *Customer records*—Examine both good and bad accounts receivables.

3. *Customer surveys*—I often suggest using a customer or supplier survey questionnaire internally as well as externally to determine needs and satisfaction. See chapter 8 for a sample survey questionnaire.

4. *Benchmarking*—Look for companies that are doing something well and learn how to emulate them. *Caution:* When benchmarking, be sure to use companies outside your industry as well as inside that are best in the world (that is, not only for the cheapest sources of parts, but the best administration, service, and manufacturing methods). For example, L.L. Bean is the best at answering phone calls and taking orders for mail-order clothing; call them and compare yours.

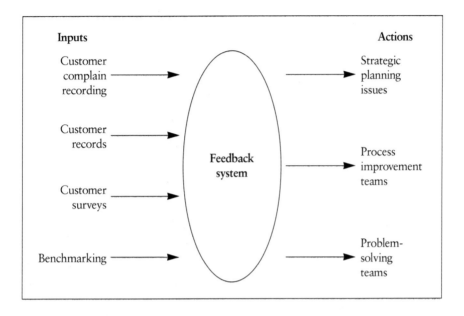

Figure 3.7. Inputs and actions to gathered feedback.

It does little good to only gather feedback from customer(s); you must do something with the results. Create an action for each improvement area identified (see Figure 3.7).

LEARNING TEAMS: CRANK UP YOUR ORGANIZATION'S ENGINE

AIM OF THIS CHAPTER

This chapter will stimulate you to change the way you think about, plan, and manage your organization with an integrated approach. Learning and sharing from each other is a worthy strategy for improved results. A learning mode occurs only when an organization's leaders see learning as something to be valued and commit themselves to it. Opportunities for process improvement are everywhere. Whether it's a solution to a problem, a reengineering project, or a product or technology to be developed—all are an exercise in learning, changing, and sharing to make processes faster, simpler, and more effective. Manufacturing companies have typically found wasteful activities consuming 25 percent of their revenues (reinvesting in inspection and rework); in service companies, 35 percent. By driving costs down, many organizations are able to recover more money than through layoffs while enhancing customer value with existing knowledge.

The implementation of learning teams quickly changes organizations. Leaders in various organizations have achieved superior results establishing learning and sharing teams. Many have realized that learning and sharing increase productivity and creative thinking. You learn when you study a process. Learning and process change occur together. *Learning is a change process, and change is a learning process.* People must learn to surrender their own egos so that the end result is bigger than the sum of its parts. Instituting organized, purposeful, and well-designed learning programs makes organizations grow together and become more nimble, energetic, and competitive. Taking time to learn and share in organizations is no longer a luxury, because the key to survival is performance and the key to performance is knowledgeable people. They should pull together and work like the fingers of a hand. Organizations must not only survive, but must often reflect on their experiences (positive and negative) to prosper and grow. Major elements of teams and their makeup are discussed in detail here.

FIXING A BROKEN BUSINESS IS TOUGH

Changing ways to perform work does not always require working harder. Working harder doesn't always work. Sometimes you need to do something radically different to achieve greater levels of success. Perhaps you have to break out of paradigm prisons, fiefdoms, habitual processes, and comfort zones.

Working smarter isn't hard. Have you ever listened to the humming wings of a fly trying to get through a window screen? The effort offers the fly little success. It is impossible for the fly to get through the screen. Nevertheless, it will risk its life trying to do so; it most likely will die on the windowsill. Yet across the room, only several feet away is the open door where it came in. Why doesn't the fly try another approach? How did it get locked into the idea that going through the screen is the only way? What can we learn from this? Trying harder isn't necessarily the solution to achieving change—in fact, it may be part of today's problem. Don't kill your chances for success; use learning and sharing teams' innovation to find other (smarter) ways of doing things. Learning teams must be seen as not only desirable, but essential to achieving positive change.

It's hard to make success happen unless an organization's culture lets everyone participate and people are not afraid to say what they think needs improving. It's okay to criticize or critique, as long as you offer an idea to do it better. Employees must not be afraid of management repercussions to suggestions. Good intentions and countless barriers keep many from incorporating learning into the organization. Management must become a catalyst for increased communications (learning). This means removing barriers in the organization, vertically (up and down) and horizontally (between functions or departments, customers, and suppliers). Management must free everyone to communicate with anyone—to say what they think for the good of the department or organization's mission.

Of course, you must maintain balance between organizational structure and freedom. You need structure to give people a foundation so that they don't lose purpose. But you have to make sure everyone has the freedom to take necessary actions as they are observed. This gets everyone involved, with people working together like the fingers of a hand by contributing themselves to the needs of the learning team. Did you ever try doing something with your thumb taped down? This is an example of four functions working together and one not participating.

Organized learning threatens traditional bureaucratic structures. Management often fears losing corporate control. Protected information and processes need to be shared. Transferring existing knowledge and skills from one level or function of an organization to another is difficult at best. The aim is to change or improve an organization's culture with management and associates communicating and moving in synchrony to fulfill goals. Everyone must become aligned with the core missions of the department or organization, with managers and associates working and learning together to eliminate causes of failure. Full process awareness and attention are required. Discussing and presenting ideas for change allows workers to feel ownership of their department's or organization's future. Realistically speaking, all encountered problems or inefficient processes, ideas, questions, and improvement suggestions are treasures and should be treated as such.

A major obstacle to maximizing productivity in most organizations is increasing associates' knowledge with which to make sound decisions. This does not necessarily mean job skills, but communication, team-planning skills, and problem-solving skills.

Too many organizations have waited until they are under competitive pressure before putting participative learning programs in place. Why wait? In the past, competitive advantage was held by those that had access to capital, natural resources, and technology. *Today, what matters is the knowledge and skills of the organization's internal workforce and how that knowledge is put to good use.* Good ideas can come from the bottom of the organization as well as from the top. Hopefully, your human resources department hired people because of their work experiences and achieved skills. Put your organization's knowledge and skills to work!

Teamwork is often thought to be an unsafe practice by many front-line employees, especially those that work to help others become better. They might not have as much output as if they worked alone. Working in learning teams requires that specific roles and responsibilities be understood and followed. Manage change in your department or organization; don't let it manage you.

Experience has found that improving end results (customer value) occurs at three levels in an organization: (1) procedural—continuous incremental improvement of daily work tasks; (2) cross-functional—improving the linkages of business processes; and (3) strategic planning—producing change, or reinventing the organization. Associates must be trained to address all three levels in the learning organization: procedurally to improve working standards and communications within their own work group; cross-functionally to participate, improve process relationships, and improve communication with upstream suppliers and downstream customers; and strategically planning to work in strategic areas deemed necessary by management, and by exploring, learning, and communicating new ways to achieve established goals. Often, stretch goals must be put in place to move associates to think differently. Creative thinking makes new ideas by dismantling old ones.

HARNESSING THE POWER OF THE ORGANIZATION

If you are going to grow, your organization must constantly be in a learning mode. To grow, you must continuously bring innovations to the organization—new products, programming, operations, and technology.

You'll survive if you have a bias toward process change rather than product change—but you need them both. Everyone wants to be the best and to become better at what he or she participates in. Don't underestimate how associates are able to contribute to your organization. Managers and associates can work together to pursue greater challenges and opportunities that contribute to the organization's growth. Everyone has the opportunity to learn from those that have been with the organization the longest, have more experience in a field, or have fresh, creative, and innovative ideas. Learning occurs only if communications are enhanced. Each and every associate is capable of continuously simplifying and learning new things that can contribute toward established missions. Learning is a lifelong, never-ending process. Helping others to learn should also be a never-ending experience for each of us. Often there is not a straight path to follow, rather many decisions to make, actions to take, and choices to be made in the learning process. Observe the paths many of us take in the process of learning and becoming a team player (see Figure 4.1).

Learning can be defined as *a change in knowledge, behavior, attitude, values, priorities, or creativity that can result when we interact with information.* It occurs to the extent that learners are motivated to change and apply change in the real world. Then they can take successful steps to integrate learning into daily work processes.

In becoming a learning, sharing organization, you must address nine areas.

1. Management must recognize that change is required.

2. Management must get all associates to understand why change is necessary.

3. The organization must have a single continuous improvement program that everyone understands and uses.

4. The improvement program must support the cross-training of all employees (administration, services, and product areas).

5. Management must encourage benchmarking, the mixing of peers inside and outside the organization to achieve Best-of class or performance excellence.

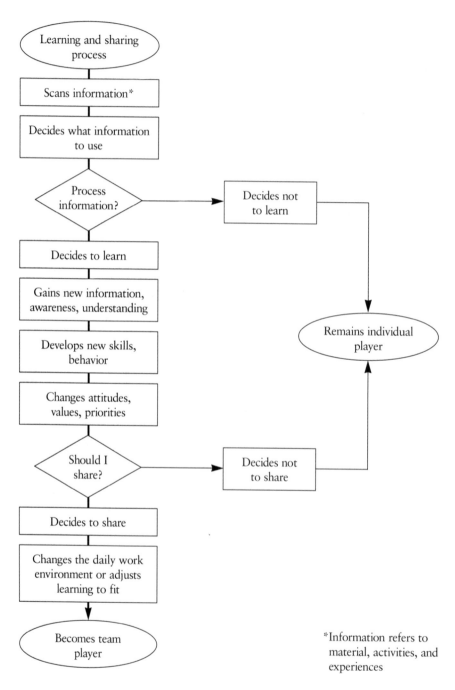

Figure 4.1. Becoming a team player.

6. The organization must incorporate outside training for new ideas and methodologies.

7. Clear standard procedures must exist, be shared, and be continuously improved.

8. Improvement efforts should be managed as projects with a responsibility matrix and project schedule plans.

9. To keep implementations progressively moving forward, activity-based cost measures must be in place.

When thinking of sharing, paint an image of a flock of geese taking turns (sharing) at the point for a while, and then settling back when they tire when flying south for the winter in a half or full V formation. You've probably asked yourself, why do they always fly that way? Science has found in wind tunnel experiments that, as each goose flaps its wings, it creates an uplift for the bird immediately following. By flying in a half or full V formation, the whole flock becomes more efficient than if each bird flew on its own. Organizations that work together, like geese that share a common direction, can get where they are going more quickly and easily because they are assisting one another. Have you ever watched a goose leave the formation? It suddenly feels the drag of being alone and quickly returns to take advantage of the flock. If workers have as much sense as a goose, they will increase their formation of teams with others headed in the same direction. Sharing effective processes makes good sense, whether with organizations or geese. Just like the single goose, no one department has ever been able to function independently for long periods of time within a total process—although many of us have felt that we could.

If a business is to become successful, its functional departments must work together. Teamwork assumes that everyone understand what visions, missions, and goals have been established. As goals change, structures will be continuously revised to meet or carry out these new directions. Enabling cross-functional process management to gain understanding of the linkages between independent functions and existing daily work tasks is a must. Let's work smarter, not harder.

■ ■ ■

One idea submitted by a learning team in the Tektronix central distribution area suggested that seven supplying divisions use a common packing slip (shipping label) on boxes shipped to them. The distribution team members wrote a vision of what the work environment would be like with only one packing slip receipt process instead of seven. Next, they created a mission statement to support the vision: "Eliminate the usage of six receipt packing slips within the next 45 days." The new mission statement necessitated communications with all seven division supplying groups. One team member said, "Let's go talk with them tomorrow." Another said, "Let's do our homework first. We need to talk to them with supporting data: types of errors made and why we make them; we need to show them what we have to do today to accommodate them."

The team documented each packing slip receipt process. A single process map was drawn that incorporated the best steps of the seven processes. It was then presented to the seven supplying divisions in a group meeting. The single process was mutually agreed on and implemented. Productivity in the distribution group increased dramatically. The project was a successful cross-functional team effort. Customers and suppliers learned from each other. How did Tektronix ever get seven independent methods of processing the same information inside one company? The company had gone through divisionalization into seven autonomous businesses, each doing its own thing. The distribution group was told by management that the divisions were their customers and to do whatever was necessary to support them. They went too far by letting each division dictate to them what they needed to perform their work. In this particular case, the definition of *customer* was misunderstood. (Keep in mind that customers always *receive* and suppliers *provide*.) If you are the customer, you must let your suppliers know what *you* need from them.

■ ■ ■

Associates (employees) must feel that they are working in a caring organization that listens to their ideas and acknowledges them. If an organization expects to be on the leading edge and remain there, it must use the knowledge and experience of all its associates. Sharing, learning together, and process ownership is at the heart of real change. *People and processes must be recognized by management as two keys for a successful change or improvement strategy.* Without it, all the reorganizing in the world will accomplish little, or will take a long time to realize improvement. If you want to know how things are going inside your company, ask the associates performing the daily tasks. Managers must learn to use their lower-level associates' brains. The redistribution of knowledge is one of the most powerful forces at work in today's organizations. But training is both necessary and costly. All the same, Peter Drucker once said, "If you think training is expensive, try ignorance."

What is your organization doing to keep your people learning and motivated—sharing knowledge, insights, and skills that reside within your workforce? Is organized learning and sharing evident as a strategy to improve your results? Successful senior managers must create a climate of experimentation and risk taking—that is, if they want rapid improvement to prevail. Your processes and the people (associates) within them are the most difficult ingredients of the change equation to manage. Associates must be able to make mistakes and learn from them without being punished. When an innovative, creative, and sharing culture like this prevails, great things can happen.

The question often asked is, Is this a self-driven process of learning, or is it management motivated? I believe associates inherently want to do a good job, but need a push (management coaching and leadership) to get started working, sharing, and learning from each other. But the most important ingredient in any change effort is establishing missions, goals, or targets for everyone to rally behind. These are discussed in chapter 6.

THREE IMPORTANT REMINDERS

1. Learn to Work Together: Managers and Associates

The skills you need—the patience to share information, the trust to let others make decisions at lower levels, and the ability to let go of existing power—do not develop overnight. In fact, in most organizations it takes between one and five years. Few companies or managers totally understand the transformation process when beginning to implement a learning and sharing team environment. Many new team leaders (existing managers) make a big mistake: They embrace the task in words only. The shift in mind-set and behavior skills that everyone must go through, especially team leaders (existing managers), is immense. Even the most capable managers have trouble making the transition, because the command-and-control techniques they were encouraged to use before are no longer appropriate. They must make a paradigm shift in their management actions.

It is essential to teach skills (build quality people) and then let associates identify and remove waste, as well as solve problems. It is equally important and possibly harder for managers to learn when to assist again, once they have let go. Too little assistance and direction is just as stifling as too much. Turning over more and more job responsibilities to learning teams causes many managers to worry whether they are empowering themselves right out of their job. But that is not the case.

Teaching managers to become leaders of learning teams is not an easy task; in fact, it's very hard. The toughest part is getting middle management to buy into the premise of trusting associates. For instance, reporting time may be eliminated, and overtime will be paid. The question often thought about is, "Will workers be fair in reporting their hours worked?" The answer is, yes, they will. When workers become self-directed, they seldom leave their work area in disarray. Experience has shown that they will work longer hours than when time reporting existed.

Understanding how learning teams work is something that you must experience and learn by sharing every day. Managers must make decisions together with associates, not by themselves. The hardest part is not having all the answers to questions the team may ask. Remember, learning team leaders don't need to know everything; they only need to know where to get the answers. They are learning too. At best, the job of the learning team leader is a blend of instinct, on-the-job learning, and patience.

Many managers ask themselves, "Am I capable of adapting to this new management style?" Approximately 15 percent of today's functional managers are natural born leaders. Then there's a huge middle group: Sharing skills and knowledge doesn't come naturally to them, but they can learn to do so. The remaining 15 percent are poor candidates to lead a learning team, because it runs counter to their personality.

If you have no idea what self-managed teams are, you're not alone. You can read books on self-managed teams and visit companies like Advanced Technological Laboratories, Hewlett-Packard, Tektronix, or Johnson & Johnson that have successfully used teams. If you have the opportunity to visit a company with a self-managed team environment, observe how associates perform the work they have learned. They participate and have more say in how daily work is performed. Observe how they display ownership of the process in which they work.

Learn from other team leaders—inside and outside of your organization—how they plan, establish goals, set objectives with milestones, and transfer responsibility to teams. Today's managers should establish a transfer project plan or, in other words, make plans for the transfer of their existing responsibilities. Plan what to transfer and when. What will they teach their learning team today? What will they transfer this week, in the next couple of months? List what obstacles need to be removed to make the associates' jobs easier. Invest in long-term sharing and establish a partnership between management and associates. Weaning, or backing managers out of their old established mind-sets, is tough. Plan for the transfer.

Here are two approaches to implementing a learning environment.

A. *Phase into teams.* Ease into a learning and sharing environment; move slowly by identifying several employees that you think might be receptive to the sharing and learning idea. Once the first learning team (group) begins working well together, expand its membership. Eventually break off some existing team members and start new teams. Be sure and explain what you are trying to do, and why everyone that participates will benefit from the sharing and learning. Implement at a comfortable speed—your own speed. Bring in an outside, unbiased person to assist you in teaching communication, interpersonal, activity-based process management, and improvement skills, if necessary.

B. *Burn the bridge.* Instead of phasing sharing and learning in small steps, as might be expected, set a goal of accelerated learning within x months. Establish a project schedule plan with your staff's assistance. Managers must make sure that everyone knows they are serious about creating a learning and sharing organization, even if it means reorganizing. Creating a big fuss all at once can prevent obstacles from getting in the way. Flattening the organization often requires a reduction in management or supervision. Make sure all associates have a place on a learning team or somewhere else to go if their job is eliminated, otherwise internal problems will begin.

2. Establish a Foundation

Strategies, annual goals, priorities, and performance measurement systems must be understood, shared, and learned by everyone. Implementing empowered, sharing, and learning teams with accountability requires four basic project planning practices.

a. Establish expectations regarding end results.

b. Measure results achieved at specific times.

c. Establish formal followup checkpoints.

d. Listen and respond to improvement recommendations made by teams.

3. Recognize That Three Types of Improvement Authority Exist In Learning Teams

Each of us has a sphere of authority within a total process, which consists of a small circle of events that we can control. Other teams lie within a circle of things within a total process that you cannot control; others have authority over them. Your functional work team must continuously communicate with other teams outside its authority, or it will waste energy and contribute to things that go wrong in a total process.

Review the various types of team authority, depicted in Figure 4.2.

Type 1. Your daily work team (the gray circle in Figure 4.2) has *complete authority* to identify, analyze, and solve problems and improve internal processes without involving outside functions or departments. These team characteristics include the following:

- You can identify and define internal department or functional improvement areas.

- You have control of the internal data collection process.

- You have the expertise to analyze improvement areas and develop solutions.

- *You have the authority to implement the internal solutions.*

Type 2. Your daily work team has *limited authority* and control of external improvement areas. Team members need to go outside of their own (gray) area to get additional external input (white area) and may have to

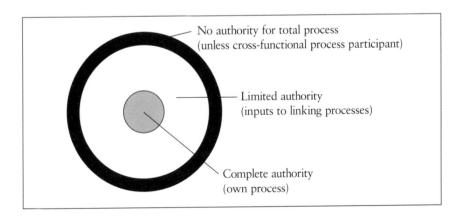

Figure 4.2. Three types of improvement authority.

get authorization from another functional or department manager to implement the solution. These team characteristics include the following:

- You can identify and define internal or external improvement areas.

- You have control of internal data collection.

- You may lack expertise to analyze the external improvement area coming from a provider (supplier) or to find solutions.

- You have limited authority to force implementation of external solutions.

- *You can influence outside decision makers if they are a direct supplier or customer.*

Type 3. Your daily work team has *no authority* over the downstream improvement areas. Typically the improvement area is beyond the scope of the internal group and must be handled as a cross-functional project within the larger organization. These projects are selected and reviewed by senior management. These team characteristics include the following:

- You can identify and define improvement areas.

- You can collect data as it pertains to your daily work tasks or department.

- You lack the understanding to analyze the improvement area in its entirety or to find solutions without the process owner's assistance.

- *You have no authority over the ultimate decision maker unless you become part of a strategic cross-functional process improvement project.*

It takes strong leadership from the top and the willingness to change the organization's culture to successfully implement a learning team environment. Commitment has to start with senior managers. Once they are on board (have documented missions and goals), the challenge is to get the rest of the organization—line managers, associates, clerks, engineers, accountants, and so on—to understand their part in creating learning teams. Keep in mind that people naturally resist change.

After all, we're asking all associates to share everything they have ever learned with others so that others can *learn what they know.* Associates are often hesitant to share with their peers or with lower-level personnel. They must understand *why* your organization is creating learning teams, not just *what* learning teams are. A learning organization necessitates creating a culture that requires increased communication and teamwork. Everyone must understand that capturing more business in the future requires increased productivity without increasing people or floor space.

Paper profits and dividends, the yardstick of many organizations' senior management, make no contributions to improve the workings of an organization. Only improvements in frontline productivity and quality do. Management must help them to do a quicker and better job.

WORKING TOGETHER IN TEAMS: UNDERSTANDING THE TYPES OF TEAMS, ROLES, RESPONSIBILITIES, MEETINGS, AND CONSENSUS

Types of Teams

When trying to use teamwork as a productivity improver, many businesses have reaped poor results. There are several distinct types, and each performs differently. All types of teams can contribute productively, but each in different ways.

Team Type A—Fixed Tasks, Working in a Series. Members of this team work individually at fixed tasks where they perform duties in a series of linking operations in which each contributes to the overall process. Examples include a traditional assembly line and most administration and service functions.

Members of this team are responsible only for their own task. They never leave their task to assist others. Work is passed on to others, who in turn perform their task and pass it on again.

Team members have clear, defined goals and can be held fully accountable for their separate task. This type of team works well when processes are well-documented and understood at each work station.

Team Type B—Fixed Tasks, Working in Parallel. This team consists of individuals working at fixed tasks, but simultaneously together. Examples include building modules for final assembly or a new product introduction.

While members of this team do not aid each other, they work as a team in the sense of performing simultaneously together. Not free to do as they please, they must follow rigid schedules or procedures for each task. This team is different from the first in that the total process must take place in parallel rather than in a series of sequential steps.

Team Type C—Fixed Tasks, Assisting Others. Members of this team have fixed tasks and aid and assist others in accomplishing overall team tasks. Examples include group efforts and work cells.

This is the kind of team most organizations are trying to develop. Members are cross-trained, work together, understand the function of each other's task, and can work wherever needed. There is one overall goal for the team, yet individual members can assist others if a bottleneck appears. The team is the real performer, fulfilling customer needs in the shortest time possible. Self-check (during the transformation) and successive check (at the next step) are an integral part of their tasks.

PITFALLS ON THE PATH TO TEAMWORK

Once a team is in place, it is very difficult to change from being one type of team to another. For teamwork to be effective, there must be a total mind-set change away from the past way of doing things. Changing from the traditional "I'll do my own job my own way" to a team approach of "let's work together" usually means that people must accept change.

It is helpful to look at teams as complex tools, and as such, they must be carefully planned and selected to meet specific improvement projects and their goals. Remember that each team type has its own uses, characteristics, and constraints.

The key to having a successful team lies in analyzing your existing needs, reviewing the type of process, then selecting a team type that supports it. Many times a combination of team types is required. For cross-functional business processes, you might choose type A and type C teams. Type A would cover the many different functions linked together, and type C would get at the details in daily work tasks. Whatever type of team you choose, you are actually beginning a new culture. Working in learning teams is a necessity for future business success. A group of talented individual associates will not necessarily produce a productive learning team.

What happens if associates do not buy into the concept of learning teams? This may seem like a trivial issue, but suppose you walked into your office one morning and it had been completely rearranged. No explanation is offered other than "It's better this way." How would you feel? Probably the same way any of your associates would feel if you changed their work environment without consulting them first. Involvement of associates should be considered mandatory in the development and innovation of learning teams.

WHY LEARNING TEAMS TYPICALLY FAIL

The history of teams documents many unsuccessful learning team efforts. The following 14 reasons for failure will provide you with things to watch and plan for.

1. Lack of a coherent plan; inadequate directions for actions.

2. Lack of leadership (direction, support, teaching, sharing, and learning) from management.

3. Titles and longevity are not left at the meeting door. To succeed, everyone must be an equal participant. The only titles used in a meeting are those assigned to team members who handle specific team tasks.

4. Unrealistic expectations of the team; team cannot influence outside functions.

5. The climate is not "right" (management is reluctant to delegate authority to do the job, and the real reason is a lack of trust).

6. No awareness of how to handle group dynamics.

7. Individual hidden agendas.

8. Problems not clearly defined, data have not been gathered.

9. Jumping to solutions (fixes).

10. Overpowering of group by a few learning team members.

11. Responsibilities are not shared within the group.

12. A competitive (I or me) rather than cooperative (we) atmosphere exists.

13. Fear of confronting unpopular issues or processes.

14. No followup or evaluation of projects.

A learning team's success requires the shared responsibility of each member. If a team doesn't arrive at a desired end result, it must share what it learned from the experience and what not to do again. Team members must be committed to the success of the team. They must try to retain their objectivity, keep open minded to others' opinions, cooperate with others' ideas, and maintain an equal position at all times. One of the goals of an effective learning team is ongoing involvement by associates at every level of the organization. Because participation is important to the outcome of team meetings, a team leader must promote, manage, and coach participation. Unmanaged or uncoached participation results in nothing but chaos.

THE TEAM LEADER'S ROLE

When learning teams are being established within a department or organization, a climate must exist in which all associates feel it is both safe and desirable to expose and share improvement ideas. The team identifies as many causes for a problem as possible in a brief period of time. Problems, causes, and solutions (fixes) are identified without finger-pointing or injury to reputations. The team leader's role, in part, is to ensure that the process of experimentation doesn't end in fault-finding, but leads to understanding and opportunities for process improvement. If mistakes are made, that means decisions are being made and risks are being taken. Companies will not grow without risk. The team leader's role consists of the following responsibilities.

- Offer sincere support for associates during their learning process.
- Teach other team members tools to visually display data.
- Guide without dominating; involve all team members in the sharing of information.
- Communicate with management: status, problems, obstacles, and results.
- Coordinate team activities; keep nonmembers that are linked to the process informed.
- Follow up on assigned action items and commitments to share results at specific milestones.
- Measure and track results.

The team leader kicks off the first meeting. A beginning statement might be, "The reason you were invited to this meeting is to get your help in identifying and solving the rejects we've been having with _____. We'll need to finish the project by _____."

TOOLS OF A GOOD SPEAKER

Eleven suggestions for making a successful presentation to learning team members and management are listed here. I encourage you to read and practice them each time you are preparing a presentation. These suggestions apply to all learning team members, not just the team leader or facilitator. Mastering communication skills aids everyone's career growth.

1. Don't read your speech or presentation. Maintain eye contact with your listeners. Relax and feel confident because you know your subject.

2. Never give excuses for being unprepared or put down your speaking ability. Do the best you can.

3. Organize your materials, present, and ask for questions.

4. Know your audience. Never talk down to or patronize your audience.

5. Make sure you are heard. It is better to be too loud than too soft. Be intense and enthusiastic.

6. Make sure your gestures are natural, sincere, and meaningful. Fifty percent to 80 percent of communication is nonverbal.

7. Make sure that the visual aids enhance your presentation. Talk to your audience, not to your visuals. Make sure the type is 20 point or larger.

8. Always look at your audience. Look at the spot between someone's eyes. When addressing a small group, look at specific individuals or the whole group. In large groups, try focusing on one section at a time.

9. Use brief examples to explain something.

10. Be enthusiastic about your subject, then the audience will also become enthusiastic. Present a positive image, and audience members will listen to you.

11. Stage fright and jitters are the rule rather than the exception. Let the emotions encourage you to prepare yourself well. Then you'll do well.

GETTING STARTED: ATTENTION TO THE SHARING AND LEARNING PROCESS

For a successful implementation of a mission, goal, or target, the role of the facilitator and other team members must be understood and assigned.

Team Facilitator's Role

- Assist in the training to use tools that will aid in the learning and discovery of solutions through data gathering.
- Provide ongoing information exchange and support.
- Reinforce necessary skills and learning.
- Advise and assist in resolving problems.
- Coordinate pre- and postmeeting notes.
- The facilitator's contribution to effective meetings means being prepared. If unable to attend a meeting,
  —Notify a substitute several hours ahead of time to give time to prepare.
  —Cancel a meeting only as a last resort; others want to share what they have accomplished and want to learn.
  —Let the learning team members know as far in advance as possible who will be substituting for you.
- Prepare for meetings.
  —Provide copies for each member of the meeting agenda and any overheads used.
  —Ensure the availability of equipment required during the meeting (television, VCR, overhead projector, recorder, and so on).
  —Schedule key speakers when it is necessary to learn from someone outside of your daily task group.
  —Start the meeting on time and end it on time.
  —Promote and monitor total participation; initiate sharing and learning with each other.

Team Member Roles

- Attend all scheduled meetings.
- Be committed to participate, share, and learn. Be on time.

- Share responsibilities and tasks with others if you are aware of the process steps involved.

- Participate—speak out during meetings. Let others learn from you.

- Listen to the thoughts and views of others.

- Complete your assignments on time. You will be measured against expected delivery dates.

- Use problem-solving techniques to identify and reach solutions.

- Interface, share, and learn along with other coworkers.

- Cooperate and remain objective. All suggestions for solutions will be tried.

- Show appreciation to nonmembers who visit the team. They want to learn what to do.

- Avoid negative judgments toward the ideas of others. Learn from them.

- No disruptive side conversations will exist. Let everyone know what you are thinking. Share.

Remember that success is a shared responsibility.

TEAM ACTIVITIES CHECKLIST

It's a good idea to follow a checklist of events that tracks who is responsible for what every time a new team is brought together to prevent failures. A Grass Valley Group working checklist follows; you may want to create a similar list of your own.

1. Define learning expectations and ground rules.

2. Review rules and responsibilities.

   —The facilitator is the group leader.

   —The team reporter records meeting minutes.

   —Determine how to recruit new team members.

3. Team maintenance.

—Practice brainstorming with Post-its and solving problems with data.

—Use flipcharts to record meeting activities.

—Publish and distribute meeting minutes within 24 hours.

4. Meetings.

—Did we start on time?

—Did we review all scheduled action items?

—Did we stick to the scheduled agenda items?

—Did we summarize meeting activities at the end of the meeting?

—Did all new items and tasks get assigned, with due dates?

—Was a date established for the next meeting?

—Was the agenda established for the next meeting?

5. Meeting minutes.

—Did we record who was in attendance?

—Were highlights/actions of the last meeting discussed?

—Were the next action items recorded for the next meeting agenda?

—Were minutes distributed to team members?

TEAM FUNCTION CHECKLIST

Reviewing environmental influences, goals/targets, roles of team members, procedures, and team relationships aids in the creation of and workings of new learning teams. The more questions answered positively, the greater the team's success has been.

Environmental Influences

1. Are team members in close physical proximity and able to meet regularly?

2. Are the appropriate skills represented on the team?

3. Are the appropriate levels of authority (internal/external) present within the team?

Goals/Targets

1. Are team members involved in setting objectives?

2. Are objectives understood by all team members?

3. Do all team members agree with the objectives?

4. Are the objectives set achievable within the time frame established?

Roles of Team Members

1. Are roles clearly defined and do not overlap?

2. Are roles understood by all team members?

3. Does the leadership understand its clearly defined responsibilities?

4. Do team members know their assignments?

5. Are team members and leaders accessible, and do they assist each other in the learning process?

Procedures

1. Are decisions made by consensus?

2. Do meetings make efficient use of time and are they task oriented?

3. Is emphasis of the meeting on problem solving, sharing, and learning, versus blaming the individual responsible working within the process?

4. Does everyone participate in the sharing and learning discussions and meetings?

5. Are minutes distributed within 24 hours of the team meeting?

6. Does everyone listen, share, and learn with everyone else?

7. Are individual team members given feedback regarding their performance on the team (that stays within the team meeting)?

8. Is everyone kept informed?

9. Are deadlines and milestones clearly established and agreed upon by the team?

Team Relationships

1. Is there team identity?

2. Is there tolerance for conflict with an emphasis on resolution?

3. Is conflict openly discussed?

4. Do team members teach and support each other?

ESTABLISHING MEETING GROUND RULES

The following 11 ground rules have been successfully used by client learning teams to develop a good working relationship among team members. While there are many ways to organize and conduct meetings, there are a few core elements that should always be considered to obtain maximum benefit from any meeting.

1. Leave all titles or positions outside the meeting. Associates need to be free of any fears of hierarchy to make the maximum contribution.

2. Set time limits for agenda items and be on time. Associates will be more driven to contribute if the meeting takes place within a known time frame and starts and stops on time. Waiting for one person incurs the cost of everyone else's time.

3. Brainstorm using Post-its. Being able to think about alternatives and offer suggestions without limits is always productive. Documenting ideas in a brief and highly visible fashion assists everyone and encourages listening. Post-its help in two ways: They put mufflers on "mega-mouths," and they get quieter people to talk.

4. Focus on customer and supplier needs, not wants. Focusing on needs avoids the nonproductive nature of the "battle of opinions."

5. When problems occur, review and share process details rather than peoples' activities.

   —We all need to understand what is being talked about. The only dumb question is the one that doesn't get asked.

   —Disagreements are okay, because they'll make for a better final solution. Learn from others' points of view.

6. Listen, listen, listen. Seventy percent of your time in meetings should be spent listening to others. Try not to interrupt others when they are talking.

7. Work for a win-win solution for all. Try to avoid having a meeting end with winners and losers. Reach consensus, do not vote. Voting divides groups into "we" and "they" sides.

8. Work with data, not "I think" statements. It is much easier for associates to discuss documented issues than an opinion. "I think" can often mean "I don't know, but . . ."

9. Make sure process documentation is updated. Most meetings are held to update an existing process that has gone astray. When a problem is remedied, process the appropriate paperwork. You will have a new standard to work from.

10. Make sure you train with the new documentation. Updated documentation does no good unless others who perform the same function are trained in the new procedure.

11. Celebrate successes. Review and celebrate successes and failed attempts. Many businesses are now celebrating the completion of projects before their end results are known. Acknowledge associates' efforts for trying something new.

HOW TO RUN AN EFFECTIVE MEETING

The productivity of a team is often determined by the efficiency of its team meetings. Ineffective meetings waste everyone's energy. Successful meetings help focus everyone's energy on the task at hand (see Figure 4.3).

Good Meetings	Bad Meetings
Content-focused (NEAT meeting)	Unfocused meeting
1. Nature of meeting—specific agenda _____	1. No clear agenda
2. Expectations—stated purpose _____	2. Purpose unclear, no understanding of issues
3. Actions to be taken—clear objectives _____	3. Objectives ambiguous
4. Time—reasonable amount of material to cover ____	4. Too much material to explore
Value-adding process	Wasteful process
1. Meeting begins and ends on time _____	1. Meeting starts late and/or lasts too long
2. Discussion orderly and logical _____	2. Irrelevant discussion
3. Ideas are well-founded _____	3. Shooting-from-the-hip comments
4. Sharing, supportive climate _____	4. Defensive climate
5. Open communication _____	5. Communication stifled
6. Participation on relevant topics _____	6. Private agendas discussed
7. Conflict handled constructively _____	7. Hostility and conflict not dealt with
8. Logical, in-depth treatment of problems _____	8. Superficial/inadequate handling of problems
Real sense of accomplishment	Frustration/illusion that something was accomplished
1. Expectations defined _____	1. Unrealistic expectations or exceptions raised
2. Results documented _____	2. Undocumented results
3. Activity's goals defined _____	3. No commitments
4. Responsibilities, steps clear _____	4. Pressure to produce something
5. Action items completed and evidence produced ___	5. Nothings happens that demonstrates change

Figure 4.3. Good meetings vs. bad meetings.

1. Ask, "Are all the scheduled meetings necessary?" Cut down on unnecessary meetings.

   —If a meeting is just to disseminate information, use memos or electronic mail.

   —If a meeting is to gather information, try using written surveys or data gathering before a meeting is held.

   —If a meeting is to gain acceptance, does the whole group need to accept something?

   —Improve meetings, don't eliminate them. Face-to-face interaction is important.

2. Prepare an agenda and insist that needed research information is brought to the meeting. Items requiring advance work should be sent early.

3. Invite only participants who have a role, purpose, or interest in the meeting. Remember: The larger the learning group, the more complex the meeting will be to manage.

4. Start on time, all the time: beginning, breaks, lunch, and so on.

5. Begin by summing up the minutes of the last meeting and reviewing the agenda for this meeting: topics, expected outcomes, responsible people, estimated time required.

6. Encourage all team members to participate, share, and learn from others.

7. Have team members list and clarify ideas on Post-its, one idea per note.

8. Tactfully keep the discussions on track; call time-outs when the meeting is straying from the agenda.

9. Aim for consensus, fully discuss everyone's ideas.

10. Assign action items with due dates to individuals.

11. At the end of each meeting, sum it up before leaving.

12. Close the meeting on time.

13. Distribute the minutes within 24 hours.

MANAGING DISRUPTIONS IN TEAM MEETINGS

Many annoying or disruptive situations will occur during your scheduled meetings. Following are 10 common disruptive situations you will confront as a team facilitator and ways in which you can address them successfully.

1. Late arrivals to a meeting

—Don't confront latecomers publicly. If being late is habitual, meet with latecomers privately and identify what's going on.

—If latecomers have reports to deliver to the team, schedule their presentations early in the meeting agenda.

—Have someone call habitual latecomers before the meeting to remind them.

2. Low team energy

—Get people involved; use brainstorming with Post-its.

—Ask for feedback: Is clarification needed on certain points? Are team members ready for a break?

—Be positive, open, and receptive to team members' ideas. Create a safe environment in which they can contribute and learn.

—Take stretch breaks as well as regular breaks.

—Make sure the objectives for the meeting are well understood. What are you *all* planning to accomplish? Explain how the result will benefit them.

—Hold stand-up meetings. Remove chairs from the room before the meeting begins.

—Polish your presentation skills. Study a tape of your voice and find ways to make it more interesting. If possible, study yourself on videotape. Watch what other speakers do and observe the effectiveness of their styles.

3. When two or three team members insist on arguing with each other, don't let it continue if it's counterproductive. Suggest that they continue the discussion on their own time after the meeting.

4. When the whole group is arguing, summarize the different points of view. Use Post-its to gather everyone's ideas, or table it for another meeting to allow participants to mull over the ideas.

5. Distractions

—Arrange the room so that people enter from the back.

—Hold beverages for the group until after the business portion of the meeting.

—Get the group to agree to hold all calls unless it's an emergency. Pretend that the meeting is being held 500 miles away.

6. Long-winded talkers (mega-mouths)

—When they stop to breathe, break in, summarize briefly, and invite the opinions of others.

—Set time limits on agenda items and on talking.

7. Negative people

—Don't argue with them or defend yourself. Validate their feelings: "I can see that you're frustrated. . . . You don't think this idea will work . . ." Then ask for other points of view from the rest of the meeting participants. Ask the negative person what his or her positive suggestions are.

—Stress the importance of holding judgment until all ideas are considered.

8. When the meeting drifts

—Refer everyone back to the agenda.

—Ask leading questions referring to the meeting's objectives.

—Suggest that new items be discussed toward the end of the meeting if there's time or that the new items be added to the next meeting's agenda.

9. When people are coming and going during the meeting

—If the group meets regularly, meet privately with the offenders and tell them, "I really get distracted when you keep leaving the room. It draws energy and focus from the others, too. Maybe you and I could brainstorm ways to reduce these interruptions."

—Have the group vote on holding all calls and messages unless there is an emergency.

—If it's a one-time meeting, speak to the person during a break.

10. Loner (hermit) in the back of the room

—Encourage the person to join you: "We need your energy and your ideas; we want to learn what you are thinking."

—Socialize with the person during the break. He or she might have good ideas to share, but is too shy to speak in a group.

HANDLING CONFLICT RESOLUTION AND ACHIEVING CONSENSUS

It is often helpful when discussing consensus to first define what it is *not*. *Consensus is not unanimous agreement*—we all have our own needs and agendas, which not every proposal will completely satisfy everyone. *Consensus is also not majority rule*—in situations where unanimous votes are a regular occurrence, usually opposing views are seldom heard. In using small learning groups, everyone's support is required for a project's success.

What then is consensus? It is an agreement by all team members to support a decision on a specific issue. To find the common ground of consensus, all team members must be able to reach their personal goals while also accomplishing the group goals. This can be done only with an in-depth exploration of different views and needs. You must look at the forest and see the trees.

Why Is Consensus Best?

The key to unlocking real openness is to teach workers to give up having to agree. Instead of struggling to erase negative feelings, we can learn to use them in positive ways. Rather than work against ourselves, all we need to do in many cases is point out our weaknesses or unpleasant tendencies in a different way. Quite often, the easiest way to get rid of a minus is to change it to a plus. Sometimes you will find it hard to eliminate negative feelings, but if you do the right things, they will come back in the right ways. Besides, why is having to agree so important? Who cares? You have to bring conflicts and dilemmas out in the open, because collectively the group is more intelligent than any one individual.

Reaching consensus is better; it encourages cooperation rather than fighting and defensiveness. People who are able to work together constructively and openly are much more productive than those who are continually on guard.

Any team can consistently experience the magic of consensus if it shares a common interest (wants to make a specific something better) and approaches problems with empathy, trust, and a learning attitude. Voting establishes a pronoun war, "we vs. they" and "us vs. them." Win-win situations require that nobody be left out. The process of achieving consensus does not require superhuman abilities. It *does* require management and associates working together. Follow these steps to achieve consensus during team meetings.

1. *Establish a climate of openness and support.* People must feel that their ideas will be valued and their suggestions taken seriously. Everyone is trying to make things work better and simpler. This climate can exist only when there is mutual trust among all team members.

2. *State your position objectively without lobbying.* This is hard at first, but will become easier as you observe the benefits. The more objective you can be, the better your chances of finding accommodation with other views.

3. *Listen actively to other positions.* It is impossible to find consensus if team members do not understand all the elements of the issue at hand. Trying to mesh many different views and selecting the best requires that you see the best in each view. This can be done only by listening. It is nearly impossible to listen and talk at the same time.

4. *Look for similarities rather than differences.* This is another way to find win-win situations. It requires a genuine openness in exploring various points of view without making value judgments. This step is best accomplished by asking questions that use the words *challenge* or *opportunity* and listening carefully to the answers— not just the words, but their meanings.

- *Present your position as clearly and logically as possible.* Avoid arguing blindly for your own opinions. Listen to other team members' reactions and consider them carefully before you press your own point.
- *Support solutions with which you are at least somewhat able to agree.* This means yielding to positions that have sound foundations. Avoid changing your mind only to reach an agreement.
- *Seek out differences of opinion.* Everyone has an opinion, which is natural and to be expected. Use disagreements to expose available alternatives.
- *Work toward getting everyone to provide support.* Avoid, if possible, conflict-reducing procedures such as voting, tossing a coin, and averaging.
- *Encourage the participation of all learning team members.* Everyone must be involved in the discussions and be able to support issues at some level.

Figure 4.4. Achieving consensus.

5. *Seek accommodation rather than capitulation.* Simply "giving in" does not help achieve consensus, because you will not be satisfied with the outcome. It is always preferable to attempt to accommodate each other's views, which requires openness. In many cases, a disagreement can be a strength.

6. *Test often by summarizing and paraphrasing.* Consensus often occurs when least expected. Summarizing can help people to see the unity in their thinking. As we have said before, achieving consensus is not easy. More tips to help learning teams achieve consensus are listed in Figure 4.4.

Understanding Team Conflict

Conflict occurs when people on the same team have different overall goals. A productive learning team must have team goals that all team members understand, support, and feel are their own. Otherwise teams will not be successful, no matter how hard the individual members work or contribute. Remember that "obstacles are what you see when you take your eyes off the goal." Goals or targets must be clearly focused on, defined, and understood. Management must help by guiding/encouraging learning teams to adhere to the following:

1. *Agree that a conflict exists and propose a joint problem-solving approach.* This might seem easy, but often does not occur. Human resource personnel working with supervisors who seem unable to resolve conflicts between associates have discovered that the supervisor may be aware of the conflict, but doesn't want to get involved. Many team leaders fear that by confronting the conflict, they will create a far greater problem within the team. They may also feel that the conflict does not really fall under their span of control or expertise. All of these reasons are understandable and addressable. Practice the following:

   —*Step into your associates' shoes* to see the job perspective from their viewpoint. This is often a real eye-opener.

   —*Listen to associates' comments;* they often reveal feelings that signal potential or existing rational conflict.

   —*Meet periodically with other team leaders.* Listen to and share how you or they may have worked with and solved a similar situation.

   —*Concentrate on the issues rather than the personalities* of team members involved. Employee respect is mandatory to successfully manage conflict.

2. *Focus the discussion on the impact of the conflict on process performance.* Conflict is never resolved long-term by blaming someone else for its occurrence. Focusing on the process's procedure will encourage team members to work together to resolve the conflict.

3. *Encourage everyone to assume some level of process ownership* by having team members focus on process performance rather than their individual performance. Each associate working on a given learning team wants to have an impact on what is taking place, even if it is a small one.

4. *Ask for the team's commitment to support the process solution.* Put round pegs in round holes, square pegs in square holes—there's no stress and no struggle. Someone trying to force the round peg in a square hole may be creative, but you know the peg is where it doesn't belong. Do what is right! If someone cannot support it, ask him or her to at least try it; if things do not work out, a new direction will be taken.

Taking the time to follow these steps will ensure that conflict among team members is both addressed and resolved. The results are always worth the effort and will benefit team members in both the short term and the long term.

Avoid the Use of "Killer" Phrases

When trying to implement change through learning teams, you are tapping into a large flow of brain power from many resources. The last thing you want to have happen is for someone to use what we refer to as *killer phrases:* words or statements that can stifle the flow of curiosity, innovation, and ideas and cause people to hold back or give up altogether. We could list many of them, such as "Let's refer it to a committee" or "Aren't we doing that now?" or "Is this really necessary?" or "We tried that already" or "Darn good idea, but . . ." or "We're all too busy" or "That's someone else's job" or "Who says so?" or "Silence!" or "We've done it this way for 30 years." However, it is more important that you become aware of how easily we all use these phrases, often with devastating consequences. Everyone has heard these words and phrases, and many people are deeply affected by them. Again, management can help by fostering a climate where killer phrases are not used or welcome. The goal is for all associates to continuously think about what they are doing. This cannot happen if anything occurs that stops the flow of ideas. The wrong word or phrase can hurt, derailing the whole mind-set and hindering improvement.

What if you say no to a suggestion or thought? No is such a powerful word—it kills innovation, creativity, and continuous improvement efforts. "Let's try it," on the other hand, opens doors and breathes life into inquisitive thoughts. "Let's try it" creates hope for change and encourages participation. Visionaries say "Let's try it" even when common sense says no.

The NIKE slogan "Just do it" should replace a lot of killer phrases. If your organization is going to be successful, you have to start transforming all the processes in which people work. As people start taking ownership of their daily work processes and begin finding and preventing wasteful activities, conflicts will automatically begin to disappear. Associates will start working together productively in the processes and aim for the same goals. Thus, they will not have to spend time worrying about whether or not they are a learning team. *They will have their engines cranked up.*

PART II

EXECUTION:
HOW TO
DO IT!

■ ■ ■

CHAPTER 5

CONDUCTING AN ORGANIZATIONAL SELF-ASSESSMENT

AIM OF THIS CHAPTER

Provide senior management with a tool to identify strengths, weaknesses, and opportunities for improvement. Focusing on customer satisfaction and company leadership is a must. Change requires much thought: the involvement of all participating process participants; a well thought-out implementation plan established with frontline personnel; leadership to direct and measure the plan; and training and learning to support needed improvements. Most companies are inclined to think everything is going well, especially if the bottom line displays positive results.

To gather overall operational information for change, managers must be willing to hear that things are not working well (the problem may be them). It's not exactly fun to look at your reflection in a mirror, looking for flaws. Next, they must bless whatever objective self-assessment tool that will be used; and last, they must involve everyone to get their thoughts on what the business should do differently. One of the best tools available today to examine where to begin your change efforts is the Malcolm Baldrige National Quality Award criteria for performance excellence.

According to ASQ, there are now approximately 1 million copies of the award criteria in circulation today, most of them being used as a self-assessment tool. In 1996, 47 companies applied for the award.

WHAT ARE THE MALCOLM BALDRIGE NATIONAL QUALITY AWARD CRITERIA?

The Malcolm Baldrige National Quality Award (MBNQA) was created by Public Law 100-107, signed into law on August 20, 1987. The Baldrige Award program led to the creation of a new public/private partnership. Principal support for the program comes from the Foundation for the MBNQA, established in 1988. Since 1988, 28 companies have won the award. The award is named for Malcolm Baldrige, who served as U.S. Secretary of Commerce from 1981 until his death in 1987. His managerial excellence contributed to long-term improvement, efficiency, and effectiveness of government.

Baldrige Awards are presented annually to recognize U.S. manufacturing companies, service companies, small businesses, and supplemental sections (in the last two years the award has been extended to include health care and education areas) that excel in quality management and quality achievement. In addition to serving as a basis for submitting an award application, organizations of all kinds use the criteria to perform an internal self-assessment. In most competitive business sectors, world-class organizations are able to achieve and maintain a score higher than 70 percent. However, a score of approximately 25 percent would be far more typical of most U.S. companies.

The award criteria promotes the following:

- Awareness of quality as an increasingly important element in competitiveness

- An understanding of the requirements for quality excellence

- Sharing of information on successful quality strategies and the benefits derived from implementation of those strategies

According to an October 18, 1993 study in *Business Week,* the three publicly traded, whole-company Baldrige Award winners outperformed Standard & Poor's 500 from the time of their winning through September 30, 1993, by 8.6 to 1. For the 10 Baldrige Award winners that analyze productivity enhancement as an annual increase in revenue per employee, a median average annual compounded growth rate of 9.4 percent, with a mean of 9.25 percent, has been achieved (NIST 1993).

Other outstanding results have been achieved by Baldrige Award winners. Here are some examples of their result indicators.

- Solectron, by focusing on process quality, has seen average yearly net income growth of 57.3 percent over the past five years.

- Texas Instruments Defense Systems & Electronics Group had a 21 percent reduction in production cycle time in 1992, with a 56 percent reduction in stock-to-production time.

- Zytec's internal process yields have improved fivefold. On-time delivery improved from 75 percent to 98 percent.

- Federal Express has generated significant savings of $27 million in its personnel division since 1986.

- Motorola's employee productivity improved at an annual compounded rate of 12.2 percent.

- The Ritz-Carlton Hotel Company has been honored by the travel industry with 121 service quality awards since 1991.

- Granite Rock's customer accounts have increased 38 percent, while overall construction spending in its market area declined more than 40 percent.

- Milliken & Company's "Opportunity for Improvement" process generated 59 ideas per associate in 1992.

- IBM Rochester had a 25 percent growth in market share.

Commerce Secretary Mickey Kantar announced the four winners of the 1996 Malcolm Baldrige National Quality Award in December 1996. They are

- ADAC Laboratories in the manufacturing category

- Dana Commercial Credit Corp. in the service category

- Custom Research Inc. in the small business category

- Trident Precision Manufacturing Inc. in the small business category

Many states have also begun to offer their own awards based on similar criteria, due partially to the small number of MBNQA awards given nationally. An example is the Oregon Quality Award, which honors companies or organizations that demonstrate quality management and quality achievement in Oregon (37 states have a similar award). Merix, Inc., located in Forest Grove, Oregon, was the first recipient of the Oregon Quality Award Governor's Trophy.

USING THE CRITERIA TO CONDUCT AN OPERATIONAL ASSESSMENT

Senior managers must plan for change in the mind-sets and mentalities of associates if they want productivity increased and cost of sales reduced. Management must produce a plan that will be owned and executed by all personnel who have to execute it. Senior management should be able to start the productivity improvement process by asking questions of employees based on the MBNQA criteria for performance excellence. The criteria provide a thorough method of assisting businesses in identifying their strengths, weaknesses, and existing opportunities. Businesses that have used the criteria to complete an operational assessment have found it a worthwhile effort. You have to understand existing problems or opportunities for improvement before you can do anything about them. Management can then create a vision, mission, goals, and objectives for necessary change and improvements that will create the required learning and sharing mind-set in the associates. Assistance from all levels is required to gain buy-in for any change and improvement.

In our workshops, we use an operational assessment questionnaire consisting of 52 questions covering the seven Baldrige Award criteria categories to aid in creating opportunities for improvement. Questions after each category will aid in establishing opportunities for improvement based on the perceptions of personnel performing business and daily work tasks and their perceptions of strengths and weaknesses. These simplified questions will create an immediate two- to five-day focus (depending on how large the operational group is) or need for senior management to begin planning workplace transformation activities based on employee feedback. The MBNQA criteria categories are summarized as follows (NIST 1997).

1. *Leadership.* Describes how senior leaders personally provide leadership and sustain clear values, directions, performance expectations, customer focus, and a leadership system throughout the company.

2. *Strategic planning.* Examines how the company sets and determines strategic directions and key action plans. It examines their translation into an effective performance system. It also covers establishing short-term and long-term plans to achieve and sustain a quality leadership position.

3. *Customer and market focus.* Examines actions the company takes to determine customer requirements (expectations and needs), to provide overall customer service, and to be responsive to customer expectations and requirements. It also covers how information is gathered to understand and anticipate customer needs to develop future business opportunities.

4. *Information and analysis.* Describes the management and effectiveness of the use of data and information to support key company processes and the company's performance measurement system. It also covers action needed to ensure that the data and information are adequate to support a responsive, prevention-based approach to quality and customer satisfaction by using facts rather than assumptions.

5. *Human resource development and management.* Describes the requirements necessary to develop and realize the full potential of the workforce, including what it will take to maintain an environment conducive to full participation, quality leadership, and personal and organizational growth.

6. *Process management.* Describes the actions required to ensure process management during design/development, production,

introduction, and the servicing of products and services. It also addresses the action necessary to ensure that materials, parts, information, data, products, or services received from suppliers meet customer requirements, and that processes are in place to ensure continuous process improvement.

7. *Business results.* Examines the company's performance and improvement methods that lead to world-class leadership results: customer satisfaction, financial and marketplace performance, human resource, supplier and partner performance, and operational performance.

CONDUCTING YOUR ORGANIZATIONAL SELF-ASSESSMENT

The goal of this company assessment is to try to identify what you are doing well, what you are not doing so well, what you may not be doing at all, and—most importantly—where and how you can make measurable improvements. Begin your company self-assessment now and become a little bit better or a lot better. We encourage you to challenge your business to take the test!

Use your best judgment in establishing numerical ratings for each section. On a scale of 1 to 10, how well are you doing?

Not doing it at all	Doing okay	Doing very well

1	2	3	4	5	6	7	8	9	10

Category 1: Leadership

This section refers to how senior leaders personally provide leadership and sustain clear values, directions, performance expectations, customer focus, and a leadership system throughout the company. The leadership section elements follow.

1. Leadership System—Senior executive leaders guide the company in setting directions and have put in place a developing and sustaining leadership system.

☞ How involved are your senior leaders in setting company directions and seeking future opportunities for your company? (This includes personal involvement, communication, and visibility in quality-related activities of the organization.)

Assessment Rating _____

☞ Are the company vision, mission statement, values, and performance expectations clear, communicated, and reinforced to all employees?

Assessment Rating _____

☞ Do senior leaders review the company's performance on an ongoing basis and use the results to reinforce company directions?

Assessment Rating _____

2. Company Responsibility and Citizenship—How the company addresses its responsibilities to the public and practices good citizenship.

☞ Do senior leaders set targets for regulatory, safety, legal, and ethical requirements in all that you do, and does the company seek opportunities to enhance leadership in the community?

Assessment Rating _____

☞ Do the company and its employees demonstrate support for the community?

Assessment Rating _____

What do you perceive as company strengths in the area of leadership?

_____

_____

Let's Work Smarter, Not Harder
ASQ Quality Press   ©1998 by Michael Caravatta

What do you perceive as company weaknesses in the area of leadership?

_____

_____

Please list any ideas that you might have for addressing leadership weaknesses or further improving their strengths. _____

_____

_____

Category 2: Strategic Planning

This section examines how the company sets and determines strategic directions and key action plans. It examines their translation into an effective performance system. The key elements for the strategic planning section follow.

1. Strategy Development Process—An overall strategic business planning process should describe how the company sets strategic directions to better define and strengthen its competitive position. The process should result in an action plan for deploying the key plan and performance measurements.

☞ How well does your company target customer needs by exploring market requirements, customer and market expectations, and new product or service opportunities?

Assessment Rating _____

☞ How well do you define hoshin kanri plans (strategic goals and their execution) including competitive environment, performance indicators, necessary resources, deployment methods, capital expenditures, and training; and how well do you review performance relative to goals and plans?

Assessment Rating _____

Let's Work Smarter, Not Harder
ASQ Quality Press   ©1998 by Michael Caravatta

☞ How well have you defined your company capabilities: human resources, technology, research and development, and business processes?

Assessment Rating _____

2. Company Strategy—Review how your company's strategy and action plans are deployed. These include key performance requirements and measures. Will your company's planned performance exceed that of your competitors?

☞ Does your company have both short (1–3 year) and long-term (3+ year) strategic plans?

Assessment Rating _____

☞ Does your company have plans for improving daily work processes, employee skills, knowledge sharing, innovation, and rapid customer response time?

Assessment Rating _____

☞ Are projections of the outcomes of the strategic planning process made and compared with competitors?

Assessment Rating _____

What do you perceive as strategic planning strengths within your company? _____

_____

_____

What do you perceive as strategic planning weaknesses within your company? (Where could you do a better job of planning?) _____

_____

_____

Please list any ideas that you might have for addressing company weaknesses or further improving company strengths. _____

_____

_____

Category 3: Customer and Market Focus

How well you satisfy your customers' needs is the single most important measure of how effectively you are performing as an individual, department, or company, and will ultimately determine your future success.

This section examines actions the company takes to determine customer requirements (expectations and needs), to provide overall customer service, and to be responsive to customer expectations and requirements. It also covers how you gather information to understand and anticipate customer needs to develop future business opportunities. The key areas of this section follow.

1. Customer and Market Knowledge—An approach must be in place to determine near-term and longer-term customer requirements, needs, and expectations.

☞ Do you have a process to ensure that on a consistent basis you collect information that will help you determine customer requirements and markets? (Try to not only determine the methods of determining data—such as surveys or interviews—but also ways to ensure usefulness and objectivity of the data.)

Assessment Rating _____

☞ Do you have a process to make sure you have identified all current and potential customers, including the customers of your competitors? (Monitoring your competitors' customers may help you gauge how well you are satisfying your customers.)

Assessment Rating _____

☞ Do you survey lost customers and listen to the reasons why you lost them?

Assessment Rating _____

☞ Do you define how key products and service features relate to customer retention?

Assessment Rating _____

2. Customer Satisfaction and Relationship Enhancement—An approach must exist to determine and enhance the satisfaction of customers and to use the information gained to improve both your products and services market-related planning as well as your customer relationships.

☞ Do your customers have an easy means of either seeking your assistance or giving you feedback (inputs) regarding the products or services you provide?

Assessment Rating _____

☞ Do you measure customer satisfaction in areas such as accuracy and response time, and do you use the feedback to improve your processes and procedures and to enhance customer relationships?

Assessment Rating _____

☞ Do employees receive training in areas such as listening to customers, soliciting customer feedback and comments, how to handle specific customer-contact situations, retaining customer data, empowerment to make decisions, and knowledge of your products and services?

Assessment Rating _____

☞ How well do you set acceptable service levels and then measure them: response time, problem resolution time, accuracy, and completeness of the services you provide to your customers?

Assessment Rating _____

3. Customer Satisfaction Determination—An approach must exist to determine and monitor customer satisfaction metrics, to use satisfaction information to improve the quality of products and services, and to improve the methods used to determine customer satisfaction.

☞ Do you make and communicate understandable commitments to both your internal and external customers; and do you revise procedures so that improvements will be translated into stronger commitments in the future?

Assessment Rating _____

☞ Do you have an approach to determine customer satisfaction feedback including what information will be sought, frequency of surveys and interviews, and how objectivity will be ensured? (How you improve determines your customer satisfaction in the future.)

Assessment Rating _____

☞ Do you monitor, trend (three years' worth of data), and summarize indicators of customer satisfaction and dissatisfaction (such as complaints, claims, refunds, recalls, litigation, replacements, downgrades, repairs, warranty costs, misshipments, and incomplete orders) by customer and by specific customer groups?

Assessment Rating _____

☞ Do you compare your results and trends of indicators (such as gaining or losing market share, survey results, competitive awards, recognition and ratings) of customer satisfaction with your competitors?

Assessment Rating _____

After reviewing your assessment ratings, what do you perceive as company strengths in the area of customer and market focus?_____

_____

_____

What do you perceive as company weaknesses in the area of customer and market focus?_____

_____

_____

Let's Work Smarter, Not Harder
ASQ Quality Press   ©1998 by Michael Caravatta

Please list any ideas that you might have for addressing company weaknesses or further improving strengths. _____

_____

_____

Category 4: Information and Analysis

This section describes the management and effectiveness of the use of data and information to support key company processes and the company's performance measurement system. The information and analysis section key elements follow.

1. Selection and Use of Information and Data—The approach to selecting, managing, and using information and data to improve day-to-day operations and improve company performance is documented.

☞ How would you rate the ease of access to valid, relevant, and timely information in support of daily operations, as well as to implement measurable company improvements?

Assessment Rating _____

☞ How would you rate the deployment of information to users to ensure alignment of key company goals?

Assessment Rating _____

2. Selection and Use of Comparative Information and Data—An approach should exist for competitive comparisons and world-class benchmarks to improve the company's overall performance and competitive position.

☞ How well do you track or compare your performance to similar operations in other companies? (In order to share efficient practices, certain aspects of your operations could also be compared internally.)

Assessment Rating _____

☞ Are comparative information and data used to keep current with changing business trends?

Assessment Rating _____

3. Analysis and Review of Company Performance—An approach should exist for analyzing data to support overall business performance objectives and areas for improvement.

☞ Do you have a method in place to continuously and consistently review and analyze data as they relate to customer-related, operational, financial, and market-related performance?

Assessment Rating _____

☞ Do you routinely review company performance to assess progress related to goals, plans, and changing business needs?

Assessment Rating _____

☞ Are the company performance results translated into improvement priorities and deployed throughout the company, to suppliers, and/or to business partners?

Assessment Rating _____

What do you perceive as company strengths relating to information and analysis? _____

_____

_____

What do you perceive as company weaknesses relating to information and analysis? _____

_____

_____

Please list any ideas that you might have for addressing company weaknesses or further improving company strengths. _____

_____

_____

Category 5: Human Resource Development and Management

This section looks at the requirements necessary to develop and realize the full potential of the workforce, including what it will take to maintain an environment conducive to full participation, quality leadership, and personal and organizational growth. The key elements for the human resource development and management section follow.

1. **Work Systems**—An approach should exist to ensure that the company's work and job design, compensation, and recognition approaches enable and encourage all employees to contribute toward the company's performance and learning objectives.

☞ How well do you integrate human resources issues (such as plans, goals for education, training, and empowerment) into your overall business plans for meeting company objectives?

Assessment Rating _____

☞ Does an approach exist to empower all employees to contribute toward the meeting of established process and result criterion objectives on an ongoing basis?

Assessment Rating _____

☞ How well do you promote, empower, recognize, and reward all employees that contribute toward established process and result criterion objectives?

Assessment Rating _____

☞ How well do you pass the pronoun test?

Assessment Rating _____

2. Employee Education, Training and Development—An approach should exist to ensure that all employees receive appropriate education and training. This approach should include a conscious plan to build knowledge and skills that contribute to improved employee performance and development.

☞ Do you provide the process education and training necessary to meet your company process and result criterion objectives, including an ongoing plan to review individual and department process education and training requirements in support of high-performance work units?

Assessment Rating _____

☞ How well do you recognize and reward both individual and team performance relative to process and results criterion objectives; and is everyone involved in the development and improvement of performance measurements?

Assessment Rating _____

3. Employee Well-Being and Satisfaction—The work environment should promote the growth and well-being of everyone, and an approach should exist to monitor and maintain a positive work atmosphere.

☞ How well do you support and monitor job satisfaction including issues of job mobility, flexibility, and retraining due to changing technology and the pursuit of improved productivity; and do you address issues of health, safety, work environment, and ergonomics (health issues relating to furniture, equipment, and lighting) as well as you should?

Assessment Rating _____

Let's Work Smarter, Not Harder
ASQ Quality Press   ©1998 by Michael Caravatta

What do you perceive as company strengths in the area of human resource development and management? _____

_____

_____

What do you perceive as company weaknesses in the area of human resource utilization? _____

_____

_____

Please list any ideas that you might have for addressing company weaknesses or further improving company strengths. _____

_____

_____

Category 6: Process Management

This section describes action required to ensure process management during design/development, production, introduction, and the servicing of products and services. It also addresses the action necessary to ensure that materials, parts, information, data, products, or services received from suppliers meet customer requirements, and that processes are in place to ensure continuous process improvement. The key elements for the process management section follow.

1. Management of Product and Service Processes—An approach must be in place to design and introduce new or improved products and services or to modify existing products and services as necessary; and to design processes to meet better performance.

☞ You provide information and services to many different customers, both internally and externally. How well do you design, define, integrate, monitor, and review customer and supplier requirements when providing services?

Assessment Rating _____

Let's Work Smarter, Not Harder
ASQ Quality Press   ©1998 by Michael Caravatta

☞ Are key processes identified and their requirements documented to provide better performance?

Assessment Rating _____

2. Management of Support Processes—An approach must exist to control the support processes of company products and service production/delivery processes and to measure the accuracy of their output, making sure that support operational performance is continuously improved.

☞ Do you have support processes in place that deliver usability of their output?

Assessment Rating _____

☞ In both day-to-day work tasks and processes, do you focus on continuous improvement of support processes? Do you solicit customer feedback?

Assessment Rating _____

3. Management of Supplier and Partnering Processes—An approach must be in place to assess the quality of materials, components, and services furnished by suppliers and partnering processes to meet the company's business plan.

☞ On a consistent basis, do you review the quality of your materials, components, or services received from suppliers?

Assessment Rating _____

☞ How well do you monitor information, data, products, or services received from suppliers; improve timeliness; and communicate your needs to your internal and external suppliers?

Assessment Rating _____

☞ How well do you assess your systems, processes, practices, products, and services? Do you do something with the assessment findings to improve products and services?

Assessment Rating _____

Let's Work Smarter, Not Harder
ASQ Quality Press   ©1998 by Michael Caravatta

After reviewing your assessment ratings, what do you perceive as company strengths in the area of process management? _____

_____

_____

What do you perceive as company weaknesses in the area of process management? _____

_____

_____

Please list any ideas that you might have for making company improvements or enhancing company strengths._____

_____

_____

Category 7: Business Results

This section examines the company's performance and improvement methods that lead to world-class leadership results: customer satisfaction, financial and marketplace performance, human resource performance, supplier and partner performance, and operational performance. All five sections will be addressed.

1. Customer Satisfaction Results—An approach must be in place to summarize the company's customer satisfaction and dissatisfaction results.

☞ Have you established key product and service measures and graphs that display company trends (such as accuracy, reliability, timeliness, performance, behavior, delivery, after-delivery service, and complaint management) that ensure customer satisfaction?

Assessment Rating _____

☞ Do you compare your operational effectiveness with benchmark trends of competitors, your industry, and world-class leaders?

Assessment Rating _____

Let's Work Smarter, Not Harder
ASQ Quality Press   ©1998 by Michael Caravatta

2. Financial and Market Results—An approach must be in place to summarize company financial and marketplace performance results.

☞ Have you established key measures of company operational performance that address financial performance: productivity, waste reduction, energy efficiency, throughput time, and use of labor, materials, capital, and assets?

Assessment Rating _____

☞ Have you established key measures of company operational performance that address marketplace performance: market share, business growth, and new markets?

Assessment Rating _____

3. Human Resource Results—An approach must be in place to summarize human resource results, including employee development and indicators of employee well-being and satisfaction.

☞ How well do your graphs or tables include appropriate human resource comparative data (safety, absenteeism, training hours per person, turnover, and satisfaction)?

Assessment Rating _____

4. Supplier and Partner Results—An approach must be in place to summarize supplier and partner performance.

☞ How well have you defined the most important indicators of supplier quality; do you compare supplier's quality; and do you have benchmarks (standards by which others may be measured) established for supplier performance?

Assessment Rating _____

☞ How well do you display trends of key supplier performance?

Assessment Rating _____

5. Company-Specific Results—An approach must be in place to trend company operational performance results that significantly contribute to key company goals such as customer satisfaction, operational effectiveness, and financial and marketplace performance.

☞ How well do you trend company specific results derived from product and service quality and performance (throughput time, regulatory compliance, productivity, NPI, service, and and so on)?

Assessment Rating _____

After reviewing your assessment ratings, what do you perceive as company strengths in the area of business results? _____

_____

_____

What do you perceive as company weaknesses in the area of business results? _____

_____

_____

Please list any ideas that you might have for making company improvements or enhancing company strengths. _____

_____

_____

Your next step will be to use the information generated from this self-assessment to establish action project plans for the future.

Let's Work Smarter, Not Harder
ASQ Quality Press   ©1998 by Michael Caravatta

CHAPTER 6

BUILDING SHARED VISION

AIM OF THIS CHAPTER

This chapter explains what strategic planning is and how to create visions, missions, goals, and objectives to support your overall business plans. It discusses how to select key core process projects, assigning process ownership, understanding reporting relationships in projects, and the use of a responsibility matrix and project schedule plan for improved communications and control of projects. Brainstorming steps with Post-its are discussed in detail.

You must maximize your current strengths (experiences) and develop new ones. Hindsight is often better than foresight. An entrepreneurial type of approach is best suited for formulating and implementing strategic change. Execution sounds simple, but it never is; a surplus of divisions, agendas, and egos makes it extremely difficult to get things done. Coming up with ideas and concepts is easy, executing them across a company is tough. You need to make sure people understand that *execution is the key* because that's what the customer sees and that's what flows to the bottom line.

Understand how to execute. Create objectives for your established goals and implement them using the five detailed activities at the end of the chapter: identify objectives, implement the objectives, establish a responsibility matrix, prepare a project schedule plan, and measure project plans. This process bridges the gap between wishes and ideas to actions and realities. It reduces tasks to manageable bites and translates the overall vision into bottom-line results. A learning organization is created, which maintains competitive advantage. The project management system keeps the ball rolling and reinforces a can-do attitude. A climate of increased communication and commitment keeps the day-to-day work dynamic and open to change.

IMPROVE INTERNALLY

Arnold J. Toynbee (1889–1975) noted that no civilization was ever destroyed by external enemies. Inner decay and lack of order created their downfalls. Companies and organizations can also suffer from internal stagnation and decay. The Japanese hoshin kanri methodology is based on the principle of pulling together those inner forces within your business to unite functions, processes, daily work, and people's thinking.

■ ■ ■

At a meeting in 1994, Roberto Goizueta, corporate executive of Coca-Cola, told his managers, "If you think you are going to be successful running your business in the next 10 years the way you did in the last 10 years, you're out of your mind. To succeed, we have to disturb the present" (Lowenthal 1994).

■ ■ ■

STRATEGIC QUALITY PLANNING (HOSHIN KANRI)

Hoshin kanri is a methodology to integrate an entire organization's business and daily work activities with its medium- to long-term strategic goals (see Figure 6.1). It helps break away from standard thinking and from the

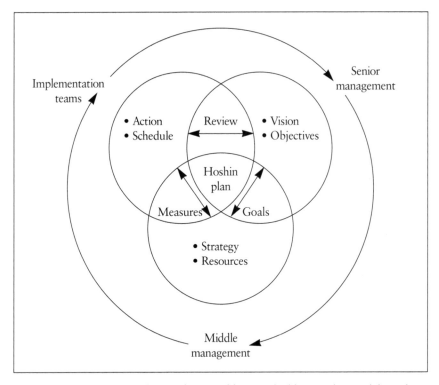

Source: Hoshin Kanri: Policy Deployment for Successful TQM, edited by Yoji Akao. English translation copyright ©1991 by Productivity Press, P.O. Box 13390, Portland, OR 97213-0390, (800) 394-6868. Reprinted by permission.

Figure 6.1. Hoshin kanri model.

status quo; it leapfrogs you ahead of your competition by analyzing current situations or problems and deploys strategic responses. It is a strategy for achieving management's annual goals (where management would like to head) through structured improvements.

Hoshin is generally translated as "the way, direction, or policy," while *kanri* means "management or control." The concept was systematized in Japan in 1962 by the Bridgestone Tire Company in response to its investigation of companies that had won the Deming Prize for process quality excellence. The concept helps you set clear priorities and find targets for improvement efforts and the allocation of resources.

Total quality control (TQM in the Western world) was just being introduced in Japan at the time, and the hoshin kanri concept was viewed as a way to pull together the disparate collection of quality control tools to form a complete methodology to meet the competitive challenges Japan was facing from the West. Most TQM methods were an accumulation of individual experiences in business and industry without any formal integration into a complete system. Hoshin kanri became one of the pillars of TQM (in addition to production control and cost control) and helped integrate companywide use of quality control methodology with commitment to quality as an overall company strategy.

Embracing the hoshin concept makes it much easier to implement cross-functional process management and continual improvement, communications, and feedback. The reason is that cross-functional process management requires a structural change in management relationships and a continuous review of goals throughout a project. Continual improvement, communications, and feedback loops are key elements of the hoshin concept and are essential to the development of realistic goals and their deployment at every level of the company. Normal verbal and written communication practices will not be adequate. Use e-mail, teleconferencing, computer conferencing, and visible procedures to enhance understanding.

Companies and organizations that employ hoshin planning will not lose their vision and insight in the daily crush of events and bottom-line profit pressures that plague businesses struggling to compete today. Instead, daily activities and processes will be guided by the hoshin strategic planning process. For employees to act on words that express strategic vision and mission statements, they must be understood as integrated objectives and measures. Richard Beckhard and Wendy Pritchard (1992), in their book *Changing the Essence,* suggest the use of *active communication* to do this. In active communication, the process is designed so that people become personally involved, building understanding and ownership. When people become emotionally involved, they translate vision and missions into what it means to them, their daily work, and so on.

Something needs to hold employees together within an organization: shared strategic vision and ownership. With the advent of the virtual organization, having a shared vision is imperative. If there is no common goal to rally around, individual goals will prevail. A shared vision provides a mechanism by which organizations remain coherent. The key is *shared*, meaning a collective, participative guide for the entire workforce.

Driving visions, missions, goals (goals are derived from vision and give the organization direction for growth and change), and objectives throughout an organization is a top-down, bottom-up activity (see Figure 6.2). The vision/mission statement that comes down from senior management as a pill to be swallowed isn't going to work. It doesn't engage the organization. Which is more likely to succeed: a company where ideas come exclusively from senior management doing innovative thinking, or 500 minds working together doing innovative thinking that deal with customers every day?

Those at the top must exhibit more leadership, commitment, and conviction. The lower the levels in the chain, the more detailed and specific the plan must be for implementation purposes. Shared vision must be a central element of everyone's daily work.

Successful strategic planning begins with a realistic assessment of the current environment, the strategies in place today requiring improvement to meet future visions, and the understanding of what it takes to create lasting change. Fundamental change involves looking at the whole process,

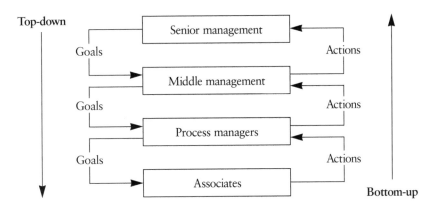

Figure 6.2. Driving common goals throughout the organization.

its functional departments, and the relationships between them. *Processes that yield undesired results are candidates for improvement.* Emphasize process improvement over improved end results; improve the process and you will achieve improved results.

The strategic planning process begins with senior managers establishing *what* needs to be improved in the business system. They must first understand the needs of their customers before the *what* can be determined. (Senior managers often identify their customers as the board of directors, stockholders, employees, and external purchasing customers.) Benchmarking how your business is performing against key competitors is one of the best ways to determine what needs to be selected as a *what*.

While the Baldrige Award criteria evaluates a company's approach and deployment and observes the results, *hoshin planning provides a method for developing and deploying (executing) for results.* The Baldrige Award criteria can be used by senior management to gather a consensus regarding opportunities for improvement through selecting three to five key core business objectives for everyone to focus on. Then you must write a strategic vision statement around which to build shared vision. Shared vision creates commitment, nurtures a nonpolitical environment, and reflects personal visions. The key product of this phase is an overall vision of what the business should be like for employees and customers and a purpose statement that moves the organization toward the vision. Ideally, the vision can be summarized by a single image or idea—for example, President John F. Kennedy articulated a vision for America's space program in 1961: to have a man on the moon by the end of the decade. Scientists did whatever it took to realize that vision. Another example of vision setting is Coca-Cola's vision directed to explicitly outperform Pepsi; its missions detail how. A strategic vision statement should

- Give guidance—a view/direction as to what your organization is going to do.

- Provide quantitative measures to stretch the organization.

- Convey a positive sense of purpose.

- Provide a unifying focus, a common aspiration of personal visions.

- Provide a long-term view or a company commitment for people to rally around.

- Be customer oriented.

- Not provide a solution to a problem.

The openness of shared vision aids in the removal of functional game playing and politics. Hoshin planning (deployment, execution, and measurement) is then carried out by middle management.

Middle management is responsible/accountable for developing how the vision's cross-functional business systems will work. Keeping in mind that cross-functional systems are harder to manage than single department functions, middle management's next step is to negotiate and select an implementation team. The team must be instructed as to what resources are available and what performance measures are going to be used.

Lower-level line managers and their employees then complete the cross-functional process team. All team members should be involved in creating, managing the actions, and scheduling the activities. Reporting occurs up through the structure to meet established objectives, layer by layer.

For many companies or organizations, this is the first time everyone has a clear picture of where the organization is going, why it is going in that direction, and how it is going to get there. Executive leadership will focus on the right things to do, in addition to providing support to employees to do the right things right. Hoshin planning requires that you establish the following:

- A *clear strategic vision/mission* of where the company or group is going that creates a common, shared picture to connect everyone together. Make sure that visions don't require rocket scientists to carry them out. The essence of a shared vision is to bring individual functional visions together in aligned harmony to support a larger vision. Eliminate the emphasis most companies place on short-term financial measures that leave a gap between development of a strategy and its execution.

- *Key objectives* that must be achieved if the business is to realize its vision/mission. Focus everything—all assets and all decisions—on your customers and employees. They are the ultimate judge of success or failure.

- *Translate* key objectives into actions throughout the entire business or organization so that everybody knows how his or her job helps the business achieve the objectives. Execute by reorganizing people and reallocating assets.

- *Fair and honest measures* (to see if goals/targets are met) so that all employees know how they have or have not contributed to the achievement of the key objectives and how they can improve their performance. Trust is based on openness.

ESTABLISHING MISSIONS, GOALS, AND OBJECTIVES

Many companies have taken great pains to design their visions; still, many don't support the way they operate. In designing visions, missions, goals, and objectives, organizations often set up task forces, hire consultants, or send executives to working retreats to explore their direction or purpose by trying to establish who they are, what they do, and how to do it better.

A sense of mission is vital to the survival of many businesses. Developing a mission statement doesn't require a huge expenditure; all it requires is time. Once formulated, it becomes the driving force of your business strategy (vision). Drafting a mission statement separates your business from competitors.

The mission statement must tell everyone who you are, what your purpose is, and what you do. Without direction, internal bureaucracy often consumes an organization's efforts, and customer satisfaction may take a back seat. Make sure your mission statement is not just a PR statement and that it includes measurable goals. Without measurable goals to support your mission statement, it may sound commonplace, or spiritless, or may even be misleading.

Missions must say more than motherhood and apple pie. Statements that use language such as "providing high-value service to our customers" and "striving to increase shareholder value" do nothing. Statements like these are transferable to similar businesses and are typically not effective. Also, mission statements prepared by senior managers only and then passed down do not work. Managers and employees must plan for detailed change together. Change must engage the entire organization. Desired missions, goals, and objectives must be commonly developed to obtain ownership and participative execution. Spontaneous change is rare.

All departments, functions, divisions, and so on must take action to move the organization toward established goals and objectives. Associates and managers alike must see and understand the long-term vision and direction of the organization and how it will be achieved (knowing that there is no ultimate answer, only an approximation, produces a creative environment). Peter Scholtes, chairman of the partnership for the Deming Institute in Washington, D.C., stated at Deming's Fifth International User's Group Conference in August 1991, "People don't resist change; people resist being changed." People will work together to implement change once the reason for change is understood. The key is to help people translate the plan into their own daily work environment.

Next, I will reference a treasury department consulting experience to explain how to establish strategic department or organizational missions, goals (targets), objectives, and measures, and how to carry them out using project plans.

Old Mission, Goals, and Objectives

Let's review how the Tektronix treasury department established its mission, goals, and objectives in 1992. Notice that no measures are associated with them, nor are there ties between them (see Figure 6.3). When asking the workforce what the department goals were that supported the mission statement, very few employees could tell me. Management had made a common mistake: associates were not involved in creating the goals. Management had created them with a "fog effect;" the employees were not

The Old Mission

To support the Tektronix treasury mission by being a world leader in treasury services.

The Old Goals

- Achieve good performance of all programs by meeting quality, cost, and schedule.
- Provide a safe, healthy, and rewarding work environment.
- Enhance role as a responsible corporate citizen.
- Performance in real terms from 1991 level.

The Old Objectives

- Conduct business using continuous quality improvement.
- Create a barrier-free organization.
- Place a priority on improving the workforce.
- Provide leadership based on management attributes.
- Make continuous cost reductions.
- Promote honesty, trust, and fairness in all our actions.

Figure 6.3. Old mission, goals, and objectives.

included or informed. Employees who performed daily work tasks didn't understand how their jobs were tied to the goals. Without employee knowledge of established goals, only management was working toward them.

New Mission, Goals, and Objectives

Compare the new mission, goals, and objectives for the treasury department with the old ones. Notice how closely they are tied to each other (see Figure 6.4). Observe how the new mission statement is customer focused, the goals state what is to be accomplished to support the mission statement, and the objectives discuss how the goals will be achieved.

Creating a Successful Environment for Improvement

Train employees in improvement concepts and methodologies, then get out of their way. The treasury department began its improvement process

---

The New Mission

The mission of the Tektronix, Inc. treasury department is to provide world-class treasury services that optimize customer satisfaction.

The New Goals

• Consolidated DSO*	60 days MAT*
• Domestic DBO*	48.5 days MAT
• International DBO	66.6 days MAT
• New customers	96% new accounts set up within one day of order entry
	100% banks and trades completed within 24 hours
• Order releasing	100% of orders received before 1:00 P.M. released the same day
• Invoice errors	Reduced by 50%
• Throughput time	Reduced by 10%

The New Objectives

• Create a cross-functional project team involving the Tektronix order processing system.

• Improve everyone's daily work processes to eliminate errors through process analysis.

• Measure business and daily work process results; post and distribute monthly. Share results with team members.

*MAT = moving average total; DBO = days back ordered; DSO = days sales outstanding

---

Figure 6.4. New mission, goals, and objectives.

with the education and training of all personnel in a workshop, designed and taught by this author, that uses the steps in chapter 9. The workshop covered the tenets of quality principles: how to create process maps; how to find, identify, and prioritize non–value-adding processes; understanding customer and supplier relationships; charting results; measuring through-put time and defects per unit; and comparing existing procedures with created process maps. (These concepts aided in the resolution of existing problems and the identification of process flow improvement areas.) At the end of the workshop, a follow-up review session was scheduled in a week to ensure that the techniques taught were being used correctly. (In most cases, if new techniques are not used within the first week, they will not be used at all.) All workshop participants immediately began documenting, reviewing, and improving their daily work tasks.

At the review session, examples of improvement efforts were shared with others. A true learning experience took place. Employees performing the same tasks were learning different ways of doing things. Others asked, "Why do they do things the way they do?" Dramatic daily work process improvement occurred in just seven days. (For example, the task of filing travel expenses was totally eliminated, creating an $18,000 annual savings!)

After several months of continuous process improvement within the treasury department, most of the easy problems were removed. Associates began running out of daily work tasks to improve. Managers began wondering, "What do we do now? How do we keep process improvement momentum going? Are we going to recognize and reward anyone?" The next step is to select key core processes to work on.

WHAT IS A KEY CORE PROCESS?

A key core process consists of a group of related departments or tasks that link together using the resources of the organization to supply a critical end result. Core process management involves the selection of three to five vital major processes for improvement projects. Senior management selected projects for everyone to focus extra efforts on (focusing on more than five core projects at any given time may dilute critical management support between projects). Projects were selected to improve customer satisfaction. Projects involved at least one of the following criteria.

- A large percentage of operational expenses
- A large percentage of people in the process
- A long throughput time
- A customer-suggested improvement project
- Something that adds value to a received product or service

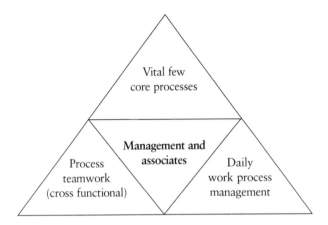

Figure 6.5. Core process pyramid.

Before beginning a core process improvement project, management must recognize that projects require a long-term commitment. (Regular ongoing improvements are in addition to core projects.) Core processes usually involve many different departments and their daily work tasks, so time and patience are required.

The pyramid (see Figure 6.5) illustrates two distinct levels of involvement: (1) the selection of the vital few core processes on the upper level that drive cross-functional teamwork, and (2) the review and improvement of daily task work processes.

To ensure that improvement continues over time, management must review measures on at least a monthly basis: customer satisfaction, internal business processes, learning, and financial results.

IDENTIFYING CORE PROCESSES TO IMPROVE

Make sure that whatever process you select, your customers are able to notice a difference when the improvement is implemented. The goal is to give customers (internal or external) the quality, cost, flexibility, and delivery they expect. At the same time, make sure the investment in improvement provides an adequate financial return. In the beginning, select only those projects that will yield the largest dollar savings; you can't ignore the financial implications. If a process is not fundamental to your company's competitiveness, it may make sense to outsource it.

Always determine why customers keep coming back to your company to buy. If you're going to compete, you must do so on quality, cost, flexibility, and delivery of your products and services. Measuring customer satisfaction is not a hard science; you delight customers, and customers leave referrals for other customers. Don't pay too much attention to one loud-voiced customer at the expense of many satisfied ones. Make sure your improvement focus is not an isolated event. You must understand what level of quality is acceptable to customers. Be careful not to set standards so high that your product or service becomes too expensive to produce.

Everyone in the treasury department was asked to complete a self-assessment based on the Baldrige Award to identify improvement projects. Numeric ratings were gathered for 39 questions based on the seven Baldrige Award categories in chapter 5. Inputs were asked for regarding strengths, weaknesses, and opportunities for improvement within each Baldrige Award category. The results were grouped into five specific areas: communications, education, benchmarking, customer complaints, and specific projects.

Five core projects were selected by senior management from the many available. It was a tough process with random voting. Since that time, I've discovered a visual selection process used by Bonnie Scherich, benchmarking program manager at Hewlett-Packard (HP) in Corvallis, Oregon. She uses the chart to perform comparisons with benchmarking criteria in HP's selection of companies to benchmark against. It uses different arrows for individual inputs from each participating benchmarking team member (green arrows = 5 points, yellow arrows = 3, and red arrows = 1). Arrows are put on the chart pointing up to represent good or positive points and are given an additional 5 points; arrows pointing down represent negative points or warning flags and are assigned 1 additional point; arrows pointing right represent neutral points, with nothing good or bad, and are assigned 3 additional points. Those participating in the evaluation process make their input by placing arrows on the chart as each criteria (we substituted suggestion for criteria) is examined (see Figure 6.6). The results are summarized, then the benchmarking process begins. A similar process is used to select core processes to be worked on, then communicating them to everyone and asking for their assistance.

Associates were asked to volunteer to work on five selected projects. Teams were identified. Their first task was to establish beginning positions; current results were visibly displayed for each project. Each project's process was then documented, charted, and visibly displayed on a wall. Every first Monday morning of the month, charts were updated with the previous month's current data and shared with all treasury members. Results from the first 12 months were impressive (see Figure 6.7).

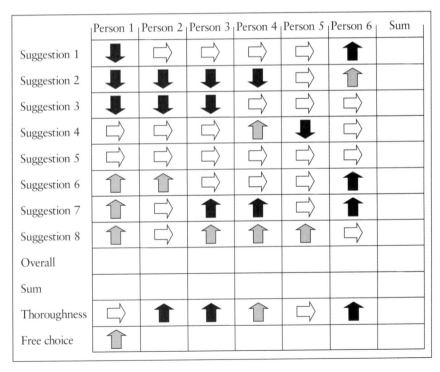

Figure 6.6. Visual summary chart.

- $500K annual savings—Invoice discrepancies reduction
- $24K annual savings—In-house systems
- $20K annual savings—Dunn & Bradstreet process improvement
- Top quartile DBO performance during 20% downsizing
- 121+ days receivables aging reduced by 25%
- 31–120 days receivables aging reduced by 15%
- 40% improvement in cash application processing time
- 100% same-day setup of new customer accounts
- 50% reduction in throughput time to process credit holds
- Reduction of 50–60 phone calls per day due to system enhancements
- Reduced collection agencies 66%
- Added toll-free phone number to customer invoices
- Increased customer satisfaction, per customer feedback

Figure 6.7. Results for the first year.

CORE PROJECT RESULTS

The Treasury department found that it could impact corporate quality and customer satisfaction if armed with the correct strategic vision of its mission, goals, and objectives. To speed up the release of customer orders by 50 percent, the credit department had to improve internal processes with innovation and creativity. The processes were reengineered with others outside of the group and existing process problems were hammered out together. It wasn't easy; barriers had to be removed. Once a core process step was improved, it was shared with everyone linked to the total process. Suggested process improvements submitted by others were added. Today, customer credit information is processed faster and at less cost (see Figure 6.7).

Reducing the number of errors on invoices necessitating frequent reissuing of bills to customers was accomplished by identifying specific reasons why customers refused to pay invoices (in most instances they were considered incorrect). Phone calls were made to customers soliciting their responses by personnel who performed related tasks. A check sheet was made from a blank customer order billing sheet. Each time an error was identified, a check was made in the specific field where the error occurred. Tim Dedlow, the treasury quality manager, found that "Getting it right the first time not only creates customer satisfaction; it also facilitates faster collection of receivables, benefiting financial performance."

The credit department now meets monthly with each of the lines of business it supports (cross-functional core process team managers) to discuss progress made in processing invoices and orders. The team members communicate results achieved and review and establish new objectives quarterly if necessary. One suggestion resulted in adding a toll-free number to each invoice, giving customers a single point of contact to get questions answered; customers could talk to someone.

Before establishing next year's goals, it is appropriate to review this year's achieved results. The treasury department's achievements during the first year resulted in improved efficiency and dramatically reduced operating costs.

CORE PROCESS OWNERSHIP AND REPORTING RELATIONSHIPS

The essence of a successful process implementation project plan is full participation. Any group or department that has a part in a core process must have a representative team member who will be included in the planning of the project to clarify activities. This creates process ownership. Equally important is the assigning and acceptance of responsibility and accountability for defect-free supplies from a work area. Open communications among all process participants is a must for any improvement project. The following procedural steps are suggested when establishing a core project improvement team.

1. Senior management selects a core process to improve (benchmark, use the Baldrige Award criteria, customer surveys, or create a list using Post-its).

2. Assign a process improvement champion (VP or highest-level group manager for span of control; a process-oriented executive who understands the linkage between value-adding operational performance and financial results).

3. Select a permanent process team (from all involved process managers or an appointed representative).

4. Establish a process responsibility matrix (for each cross-functional core process or single department/silo).

5. Create a project plan (schedule) with completion dates (everyone together).

6. Document the current process.

7. Establish measures for customer satisfaction, internal business processes, learning, and financial results.

As mentioned, all problems uncovered in the process, ideas, or suggestions must be looked at as opportunities for improvement or "treasures." These steps will avoid the pitfall of attacking only parts of processes or hot problems—set a strategic goal to improve a particular process, product, or service. Get its performance up to where you think it should be (your established goal is met). You must improve the documentation standard. Do not pull everybody off an improved process and move them on to another. If you do, the process you just improved will usually deteriorate back to where it was, thereby effectively canceling the improvement. You do want continuous process improvement in your organization, don't you? Establish new process measures and assign team members to an *additional project*. Reward and thank people publicly for a job well done.

DETAILED CROSS-FUNCTIONAL CORE PROCESS MANAGEMENT ROLES AND RESPONSIBILITIES

Senior management, process owners, process managers, daily work team members, and the quality support group all have independent and yet interrelated roles and responsibilities in cross-functional core process improvement projects. Successful projects have both vertical management and horizontal process owners that must work in unison to implement them.

Senior management is responsible for

1. Identifying three to five core processes that, if improved, will improve operating performance

2. Assigning a process owner for each of the core processes selected

3. Empowering process owners' improvement activities

4. Establishing TTT, DPU, and result measures that will be reported at least once a month

5. Removing obstacles that get in the way of the improvement process

6. Reviewing measures and communicating progress to the rest of the organization

Process owners (process improvement champions) will

1. Identify process team members for their project. All managers (or a representative) of interconnecting processes should be involved in the project.

2. Be responsible for leading the process team. Specifically, they will manage the project details.

3. Resolve conflicts and remove obstacles that get in the way of progress.

4. Prioritize improvement opportunities and efforts of the project team.

5. Report process improvement results to senior management.

Process managers will

1. Create a barrier-free environment between themselves and other managers. They will provide whatever information is necessary to each other.

2. Empower daily work team members that report to them. Daily work team members will provide whatever documentation is requested.

3. Lead the process team within their own area. They will document improvement areas, identify opportunities of improvement, and implement change.

4. Measure their work processes (customer satisfaction, internal business processes, learning and financial results on a monthly basis).

Daily work team members will

1. Contribute to the total process results.

2. Identify opportunity areas within their control.

3. Identify opportunity areas with their suppliers.

4. Survey their customers for improvement areas.

5. Support the process team's efforts with their knowledge and skills.

The quality group will

1. Provide process management tools and techniques.

2. Coordinate training requirements of project members.

3. Provide consulting assistance.

DO IT! CREATE OBJECTIVES FOR MISSION STATEMENTS AND IMPLEMENT THEM

Improving processes with creativity and innovation involves a different approach than finding and fixing problems. A problem does not have to exist; only the will to improve what you are receiving or providing is necessary. What you are doing and what you are providing to downstream customers is what you can change. Hopefully, management has already established strategic stretch goals to support your learning organization's mission statement. By doing so, management can force associates to explore other methods of performing their daily work functions. If associates are required to stretch far enough, they will have to use new processes or techniques. Management must send a message to every manager and associate that each is important and the company wants each to grow within the organization. How you do this isn't critical.

The following five activities provide a structure for planning and implementing your mission and goals through learning teams (the time displayed in the brackets is the minimum planned time for the step).

Activity 1: Identifying Objectives

Each project team member must work toward established objectives that support the group's core mission and goals.

Step 1. (15 minutes) Based on the strategic mission statement and goals for the project, each team member will generate a list of his or her top three objectives for accomplishing stated goals. (On Post-its, write one specific and quantifiable task for improvement per Post-it. Be sure to include your initials on each Post-it for later reference.)

Step 2. (20 minutes) Share with each other the written objectives in step 1. Each person will read his or her three objectives to others (no discussion takes place at this time). Place each Post-it on a wall or flipchart after it is read. Stack duplicates on each other if other associates make the same suggestions.

Step 3. (20 minutes) Share what is written on all Post-its as a group. People will discuss the Post-its with their initials on them while the others listen. Ask those that have Post-its stacked below the first one if their explanations concur. Listen and learn from each other. Understand why the associates selected what they did.

Step 4. (20 minutes) Agree on the top three to five objectives submitted by everyone. Rank them one through five, one having the highest priority, or use the chart in Figure 6.6.

Activity 2: Implementing the Objectives

Identifying all the small tasks or events involved in a process takes task understanding. (When people in the organization recognize that nobody has all the answers, it liberates the organization's creativity.) It is helpful to first lay out all the high-level tasks visually on a wall or flip chart. Then arrange them in groupings that relate to their processing or flow. Create a visual display of the activities and establish the timing for all tasks. These events and their timing will be used later when you establish a project schedule plan.

Step 1. (15 minutes) Write each of the three to five objectives identified on Post-its that were selected in activity 1, step 4, on a separate piece of flipchart paper and post them around the room.

Step 2. (20 minutes) Create focus on one objective at a time. Ask team members to share (list) all activities they can think of that impact this objective on separate Post-it notes. You may not have sufficient data on hand and have to gather it (that is, if all team members agree it is necessary, develop a survey, conduct downstream customer interviews, conduct upstream supplier interviews, analyze data, and so on; take time to do so).

Step 3. (10 minutes) Together, share/discuss the activities, one at a time, that everyone has listed on Post-its. Discard any duplicates.

Step 4. (25 minutes) Together, arrange the activities listed on the Post-its in an implementation sequence (arrange them in a linear line or in parallel as necessary).

Step 5. (15 minutes) Decide the timing (how long it will take to perform each task) for each activity identified, write the time in days on each Post-it.

Step 6. Complete steps one through five for each of the remaining objectives listed on the remaining flipcharts.

Activity 3: Establishing a Responsibility Matrix

Various team members will be responsible for task completion identified in activity 2. To document who will be responsible for what, a responsibility matrix will be used.

■ ■ ■

In a project management workshop conducted by Ron LaFlure, president of Project Management Assistance Co., Inc., he emphasized the overriding importance of communications: "Make sure that *everybody* within the project communicates with one another. Use a responsibility matrix and a project schedule plan. Without open communications, chances of failure are increased dramatically."

■ ■ ■

Write each learning team member's name in a responsibility block. When completed, the matrix document will visually display project authority and communications required among all project participants. It also identifies all the collaborating parties within the project that represent various functions, departments, or groups. Together, assign responsibility for each Post-it developed in activity 2. Steps to developing a responsibility matrix include the following.

Step 1. (5 minutes) List all responsible project participants (representatives) in blocks along the left side of a matrix worksheet (see Figure 6.8, number 1). Often it is helpful to list relevant people outside of the project team that need to be communicated with. For instance, you may need to spend money; who approves this?

Step 2. (10 minutes) List the main activities or events of the project in their sequence of implementation established earlier in activity 2, step 4. They will be listed along the bottom of the worksheet, from left to right, in sequential order (see Figure 6.8, number 2).

Step 3. (10 minutes) At the intersection for each event listed along the bottom of the worksheet, assign a responsible team member for all communications within that event block. As a group, identify them with a dot-within-a-circle ⊙ (see Figure 6.8, number 3).

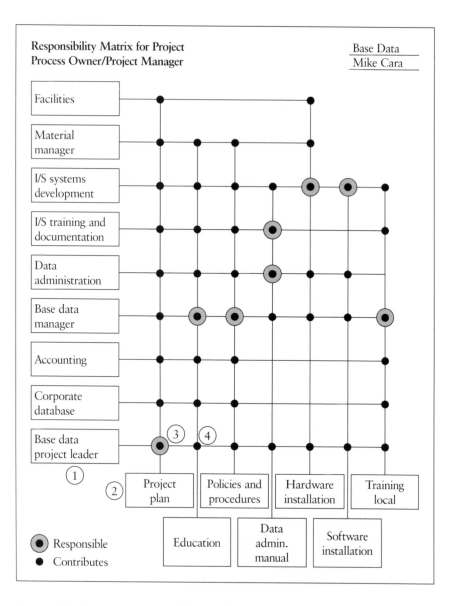

Figure 6.8. Example of a responsibility matrix.

Step 4. (15 minutes) People that need to contribute or be communicated with before decisions are made regarding a specific event are identified with a dot ●. These are members of subteams. Those not involved with a particular activity or event of the project will not have a dot placed where the lines intersect (see Figure 6.8, number 4).

Step 5. (15 minutes) Copy and distribute the responsibility matrix to all team members and other relevant people before leaving the meeting, if possible; if not, distribute it within 24 hours.

Activity 4: Preparing a Project Schedule Plan

A listing of all the building blocks (milestones) to accomplish the objectives established in activity 3, step 2 will be used. Create a planned to-do list of events that must be controlled. The project schedule plan records activities that are assigned and monitors accountability for quantifiable goals and deadlines. The plan documents aims and objectives, project team members, specific responsibilities for each task needed to finish the project, and a complete timetable. It is used to monitor daily, weekly, and monthly progress toward strategic initiatives and is updated regularly. To simplify understanding, the project schedule plan can be thought of as a road map: it shows the destination (objective), the roads that must be traveled (sequence of events), and the mileage (duration of activities). If you are familiar with the vehicle (the process owners), you will also know by looking at the map the amount of time each leg of the journey will require (individual times for each event) and when you will arrive at your destination (plan completion). Project plan elements include the following:

- *Item description* is a listing of all the building blocks or events (the road map) necessary to meet the process improvement objectives. Begin by listing the project activities or events in as close to chronological order as possible (see Figure 6.9, number 1).

- *Person assigned* is a responsible resource person who will ensure completion of an event or activity. The same person identified on the responsibility matrix is written here. Subordinate events can be assigned to other responsible associates (see Figure 6.9, number 2).

Project Schedule: Base data implementation									
Item description ①	Person assigned	Sept.	Oct.	Nov.	Dec.	Jan.	Feb.	Mar.
1. Implementation (project) plan	② Mike C.			③				
2. Education	Ron H.							
—Base data	Linda R.							
—MRP principles	Mike C.							
—Mas II concepts	Mike C.							
—Mas II bill of materials	Mike C.							
—BOM costing	Rhonda F.							
3. Policies and procedures	Ron H.							
—Corporate change control	Rich M.							
—Temporary component	Mary M.							
—Part status	Rich M.							

Figure 6.9. Example of an improved project schedule.

- *Timelines* are the tools through which the sequencing of events are affected. With the exception of most simple projects, sequencing can be extremely complex. Every project must have a planned completion date that is identified on the first line of the project schedule plan (see Figure 6.9, number 3). Draw a black line from the beginning to the end date of the project. Next, list all the other events that are subordinate to the main events. This creates an increasingly detailed work plan. These events may have subdetails listed under them. A timeline should identify the earliest and latest dates at which an event can begin and end, without impacting the completion date. Timelines should always be established as a team event. Use Post-its to brainstorm.

Follow these steps to simplify preparation of the project plan.

Step 1. (30 minutes) Pass out 10 to 15 Post-its to each participant. Ask each participant to list all activities (one per Post-it) that he or she sees occurring in the project under activity 3, step 2, listed activities or events. List all the subactivities or events in the project in their sequence of implementation.

Step 2. (20 minutes) Ask participants to share their suggested, listed subactivities with the others, one person talking while others listen, putting similar activities (Post-its) on top of each other.

Step 3. (20 minutes) Group activities (Post-its) into subgroup sequences in the order they will be implemented (many will be in parallel).

Step 4. (20 minutes) Assign approximate times for each event to be completed, and by whom. (Each group's responsible manager must concur with establish goals and objectives to be achieved with staffs and subordinates.) Draw a start and completion line on the project schedule plan.

Activity 5: Measuring the Project Plans

When followed, the steps in the four previous activities gain buy-in to the strategic plan and provide a management tool for meeting project due date commitments. Businesses and organizations today cannot afford to accept improvement delays. Measuring progress does not have to be complicated. I suggest the following:

- Meet weekly (at the same time each week) to share and learn of progress made; monitor and compare calendar dates against item completion due dates.

- Reassign priorities if necessary (if due dates are not met).

- Review those items that must be completed before the next step can start.

Consistent communication throughout a company is a necessity. If everyone understands the strategic goals and objectives—what's acceptable and what's not—a business can make rapid change. Vision awareness is critical. You've probably heard the story of a visitor walking through a granite quarry and observing workers performing their daily work. Two in particular were observed working side by side. Sweat was dripping off each of them; one looked as if he was in misery and the other had a smile on his face. Curious to find out why one was smiling and the other not, the visitor walked up to them and asked, "What are you two doing?" The first worker said, "What does it look like, I'm breaking this rock into building blocks." The other worker responded, "I'm preparing blocks for a new cathedral." The message is this: If workers are focused on a vision and understand how their work adds value, commitment to the end result comes more easily. You must find a balance between the needs of employees and organizations—balance that enhances productivity and performance while reducing operating costs.

CHAPTER 7

PROCESSES: MAKING THEM COME ALIVE

AIM OF THIS CHAPTER

The aim of this chapter is to define what a process is, how to document it, and how to review activities for wasteful events (anything that adds no value to a product or service). Visual process documentation provides a base for simplifying or removing non–value-adding activities. Process documentation gives meaning, understanding, and purpose to people's efforts.

The dictionary defines a process as a series of actions or operations leading to or contributing to an end result. My definition is broader: *A process is any activity, that resides in a department, group or organization and receives an input from an internal or external supplier, transforms it by adding value, and provides an output or end result to an internal or external customer.*

If processes and their supporting procedures are correct, you can do things right, the first time every time.

PROCESS ELEMENTS

I've said before that processes are a key fundamental element (at the operational level) of any business. W. Edwards Deming was often quoted as saying, "If you cannot define your process, you do not know your job. Everyone changes (improves) something, and that's the process in which they work." There are four key elements of any particular process: transformation, inspection, transportation, and storage.

- *Transformation* is the processing of information, data, materials, products, or services into end results. It includes any assembly or disassembly required and all other value-adding activities. In many businesses and organizations today, transformation unfortunately includes many non–value-adding steps such as inspection, rework, and doing things that are unnecessary. These steps must be eliminated for efficient, productive operations.

--- ■ ■ ■ ---

An example of doing things that are unnecessary occurred during preparation of one family's holiday dinner. Junior sees Mother trimming both ends off the ham before putting it in the roaster pan. He asks, "Why did you do that?" Mother replies, "Because Grandma always did." Junior then goes and asks Grandma why she trimmed both ends off the ham before cooking it. She said "Oh, that was to make it fit in my pan!" How many process "traditions" in your group or organization could be eliminated?

--- ■ ■ ■ ---

- *Inspection* is the comparison of an end result to the expected result. If you understand and use self-check and fail-safe techniques, inspection functions can be drastically reduced or eliminated.

- *Transportation* includes moving things about and changing location or position. Eliminating excessive activities and material handling has a large payback. According to Shigeo Shingo, the father of Toyota's production system, excessive movements can cost the average business up to 36 percent of its processing dollars.

- *Storage,* or queue (wait) time, is any time lapse that occurs when none of the other steps is being performed. In his book *Workplace Management,* Taiichi Ohno (1988) states that any time you store something, it puts your materials, labor, and dollars to sleep. Strive to keep things moving as much as possible.

Of these four key elements of a process, transformation is the only value-adding element, but in the form of rework it is also a wasteful activity. The rest—transportation, inspection, and storage—often add unnecessary costs and are candidates for reduction/removal once identified in a process.

WHY DOCUMENT WHAT YOU DO?

Task documentation provides a road map toward improvement. In essence, the procedure will demonstrate the steps you take to achieve success. This is no small concept that, once understood by operational employees, will result in a huge benefit, not only to them but to your business. Documenting tasks also has many positive side effects. It lets you share information with others, shows the purpose of what you do (are you always adding value?), provides information for others, shows who is responsible for a process, and shows who is doing the work. In addition, it sets the stage for identifying non–value-adding activities and for solving problems. Once a process is visually documented, it is much easier to zero in on steps that have non–value-adding loops. Documented processes can

- Provide confidence that you are doing the right things right—doing them correctly and in a timely manner at the right time.

- Make the steps involved easier to review, rather than forcing you to rely on information stored in your mind only. Most people know their own jobs better than anyone else—all the small, incremental steps they take to accomplish whatever it is they are doing. In many cases, however, this does little to communicate the process to anyone else. Undocumented processes make it very difficult to isolate and examine problems, much less correct them.

- Enable you to get the same output or results each and every time. When procedures are followed, results are predictable and variances will be few. The goal is sameness—getting the same results over and over again.

- Lend themselves more easily to the efficiencies of terminals and displays. Today, processes can be documented, displayed, and disseminated via computer. This enables a single database or reference point, instant recall, simultaneous display in all areas of an office or plant, and easy maintenance with changes reflected on all displays. No out-of-date documentation will exist.

- Visually assist you in identifying and removing process defects. The impact of reducing defects per unit is enormous. It shrinks throughput time, reduces the amount of paperwork or materials in the work area, and reduces the amount of rework and repair. All this leads to reduced costs.

During a flow management workshop for a division that makes metal probe tips, I asked for a process map of the current flow for review. It didn't exist. One of the company's managers volunteered to draw the flow on an overhead for display and review.

The high-level flow map shown in Figure 7.1 was proudly provided by a 25-year manufacturing manager to demonstrate how the product "moves through three distinct departments and administration functions, each managed by a separate manager." The documented process flow was analyzed by workshop participants while it was presented. The process flow discussion follows (I knew that participants would easily find inefficiencies from my visual tour).

The process begins with raw materials received on the dock, inspected, moved into the stockroom (where they wait), released by a scheduler, moved to the first machining area where parts are produced, then moved to the degreasing area.

In the workshop, the following dialogue then took place: A machinist said, "you forgot the second machining process." The process manager responded with, "When did we start a second machining process?"

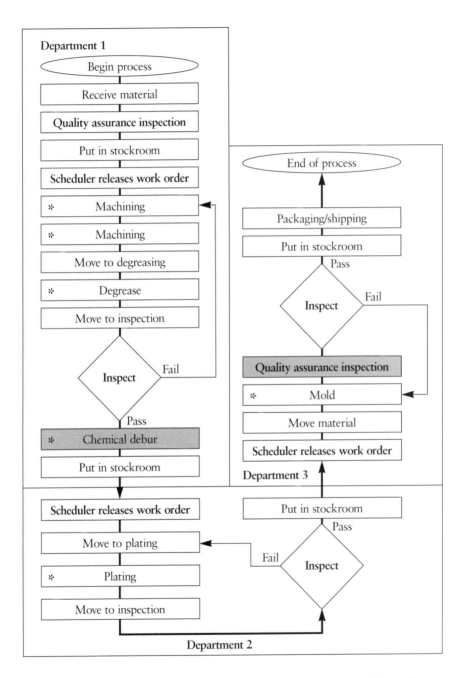

Figure 7.1. Administration and manufacturing working together to build a probe tip. Bold lettering identifies administration activities in the process.

The machinist answered, "When the tooling broke and was not approved for replacement." The tooling was replaced four days later, due to the visual impact the process flow diagram provided. Others in the audience then quickly pointed out two other activities left out of the manager's flowchart: chemical debur and in-house inspection (shaded areas). Machined parts then moved through degreasing, an inspection step (full-time administration person inspecting whether parts passed or failed specifications), to deburring, stocked again (waiting again), then scheduled for plating. Another final inspection step occurred (another administration person), and parts were put into a stockroom (waiting again) in the second department. Another work order was released by another scheduler (admin) and material was moved to the next step, molding, in the third department. Molded parts were then inspected twice, once by the operator and again by another full-time administration person, and parts were put into a stockroom (waiting again), then packaged and shipped when a customer order arrived.

After studying the flow of this process, the audience was asked to identify the value-adding steps with an asterisk: machining, degreasing, chemical debur, plating, and molding. I then asked a key question: How much time would it take to make 100 probe tips using only the identified value-adding steps? An estimate to produce 100 probe tips was eight hours. The three schedulers were then asked, "What's the total manufacturing resources planning lead time in the MRP system for the three areas? They responded with "We don't know, but can go look it up." "Twenty-five days." This meant that 24 days could be classified as wasteful activities in both administration and product areas!

While these numbers are influenced by other factors, they pointed to a fairly large potential for eliminating non–value-adding activities. First, inspection steps were eliminated by training the people performing value-adding steps to use precontrol measures and chart their own results.

The rework arrows pointing backward toward the beginning of the main process flow signaled the process improvement areas, and all other areas not identified with an asterisk became projects for removal. Just think, three salaries removed from the process in the second day of review. The last throughput time measurement showed a reduction of eight hours, a substantial two-month improvement.

CREATING PROCESS DOCUMENTATION

Two basic types of flow diagrams are used to display a process flow: a straight-line diagram, and a U-shaped diagram if you need more room on a single page (see Figure 7.2). Both share a common main flow (indicated with a heavy line), which plays an important role in identifying what should be taking place and what items are candidates for elimination or simplification. The main flow line should show what occurs the most often—what the main flow of the process is. If everything is going well during processing the flow follows this line. The side flows (thin lines) usually consist of returns, rework loops, or little-used paths and indicate areas for improvement. There should not be loops pointing backward in a process.

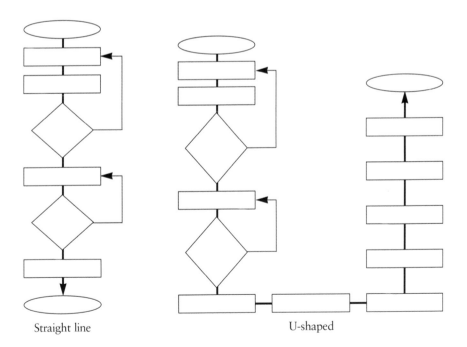

Straight line   U-shaped

Figure 7.2. Typical process flowchart styles.

Typical flowcharting is often done by choosing from as many as 35 available symbols used to completely document a process. I normally use only three: an oval, a rectangle, and a diamond.

- The *oval* signifies a beginning or ending point and is usually labeled only with a title or name. It contains no action words. Whenever you are reviewing a flowchart, look for this symbol as a beginning, ending, or connecting point with other linking processes.

- The *rectangle* indicates process steps, with a verb describing what is happening.

- The *diamond* indicates a decision/action point and should always ask a question: What decisions/actions should be taken; what are the choices? A decision/action point has a single path in and several paths out, although it can include any number of paths out (see Figure 7.3), if necessary, by using more than one diamond with a bridge.

Rework loops resulting from a decision/action usually move backward graphically toward the beginning of the process and point directly at the process step that needs attention.

When documenting a process, it is helpful to look at it in terms of three broad areas: (1) your customers; (2) yourself; and (3) your suppliers. Your customers include anyone to whom you provide something: material, information, data, product, or service. Next is yourself: what you do, your daily tasks, and your process steps. Your suppliers include anyone who provides something to you: material, information, data, product, or service. Thinking about processes in this way helps to categorize questions you will be asking about information that is key to your success.

Questions to ask customers include the following:

1. Are we providing correct data?

2. Is it on time?

3. Is it complete?

4. Is it accurate?

5. Is it more than required? (Ask them!)

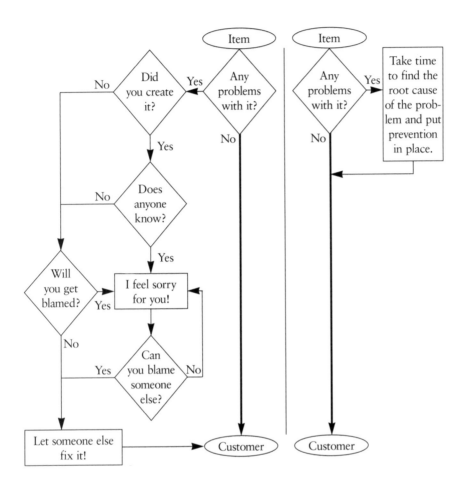

Figure 7.3. How are you preventing problems in your organization?

Questions about your own work tasks include

1. Are any steps taking too long?

2. Are any steps missing, duplicated, or out of sequence?

3. Are there any non–value-adding steps? Any rework or inspection loops?

4. Are there any delays in process? (Remove them!)

Feedback to suppliers includes

1. Are there any missing items or missing data?

2. Are deliveries on time?

3. Are materials okay?

4. Does everything meet specification?

5. Are there any incomplete items? Wrong items? (Tell them!)

When reviewing existing process documentation in many organizations, I typically see many "do-this" action steps; but few, if any, decision/action steps are identified. Without decision/action steps, there isn't a process to follow when problems are encountered. This forces you to go to the person who trained you and find out how to proceed when a problem is encountered. A documented decision/action loop enables you to proceed on your own. It is almost impossible to cross-train others, or the training time will be very lengthy—months or years—if decisions and actions aren't included. Another problem is that decisions become gray areas, subject to interpretation, rather than simple black-and-white issues.

Many processes eventually reach the stage of being so highly refined that no decisions/actions are required, but they will have many built-in fail-safe or prevention steps to stop problems from occurring.

EXAMINING PROCESSES IN DETAIL

Once a process is fully documented, you can look for the value-adding steps. Highlight only those steps that in your experience add value. The remaining steps then become candidates for closer study and possible removal from the process.

With documented processes, it is easier to confidently choose what to remove. Start by identifying all the inputs and outputs (who you receive something from or give something to) and any other connections to the process. Look to see if everything appears to be in the correct sequence, then try to find points in the process where you can measure activities before they leave or get handed off to another process.

Determine whether the handoff is negotiated or simply happens. In other words, are you receiving feedback when parts move from your process to downstream customers so that improvements can be made when something is not acceptable? Or are you simply passing something on with the expectation that someone downstream will catch any mistakes made? Only when fail-safe techniques are in place can items be passed downstream without feedback—and this will occur only when proper measures are in place. Any changes to the process, however, will always require, at the very least, an initial feedback from your customers.

■ ■ ■

During the late 1980s in a Tektronix network display division, customers were complaining that not all items were being included with their orders. Dave Coreson, the manufacturing operations manager, said that the solution was "to put a fail-safe procedure in place to prevent the shipping package from being sealed unless all items are included." To do this, a bar-coding system was implemented to (1) attach a bar code on the customer order that contained all items required, (2) attach a bar code on all items required for the order, in the packaging area, and (3) display the contents included in the customer order on a television monitor. As each item was read, the display highlighted that item, providing a visual indication for the packaging person to see if anything was left out. Unless each item in the shipping package was confirmed and included by the bar code reader, it would not allow the sealing machine to seal the shipping container in the next operation. This resulted in zero defects in shipping orders.

■ ■ ■

DOCUMENTING YOUR OWN TASKS

We suggest using a four-step procedure to document tasks.

1. Draw a high-level chart (see Figure 7.4).

2. Select (break down) one activity from it (see Figure 7.5).

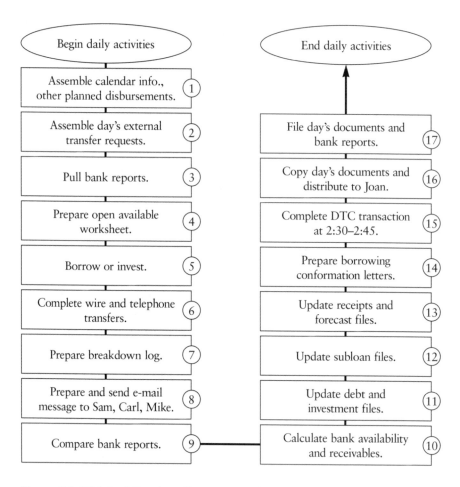

Figure 7.4. High-level flowchart: Treasury operations.

3. Look for small-step, incremental improvements you can make to that activity.

4. Keep breaking down the process to smaller and smaller tasks, like peeling an onion one layer at a time.

The high-level chart shown in Figure 7.4 has 17 steps with a main flow (heavy line) through all activities. No decision points are used at this level; it is just a list of all daily activities. For explanation purposes a "pull bank reports" task was selected as a breakdown from the high-level chart.

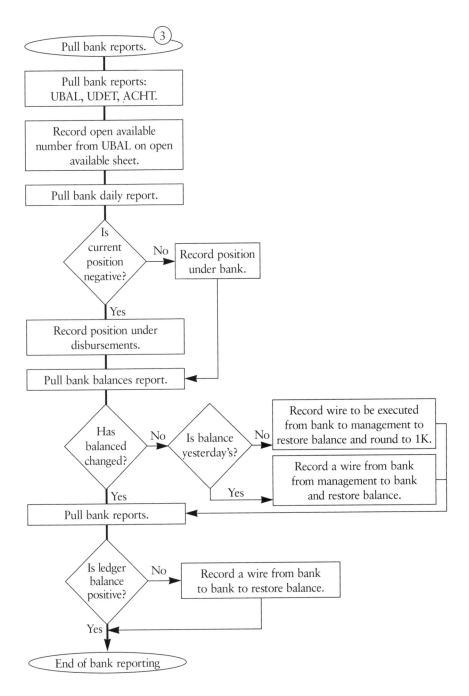

Figure 7.5. Breakdown of flowchart: Treasury operations 3.

The breakdown chart in Figure 7.5 contains enough detail to explain to somebody else in the work group what gets done. Each one of the steps on the breakdown chart could also be broken down into finer detail so that someone else could do the job by following the chart. Tasks must be broken down until all necessary details are understandable by others.

Another key reason for documenting tasks is to support ISO and QS-9000 registration, as well as government regulations (which will often consist of flowcharts with process steps listed to the side). These regulating bodies require evidence that things are under control within your group or organization. This means you must have documentation for all tasks, and the documentation must be followed. In fact, you will be audited periodically by the certifying organization to compare what you actually do and what your documentation says you do.

YOU CAN SEE PROCESSES COME ALIVE!

Have you ever watched your son or daughter squeeze a pen, pencil, or crayon tightly between his or her little fingers and try to make a picture by connecting the numbered dots in a dot-to-dot workbook, only to find that the resulting picture resembles snarled fish line? The first dot was connected to the fifth dot, the fifth dot was connected to the third dot, and so on. You ask "Why didn't you follow the numbers in numerical order, the one to the two, the two to the three, and so forth, the way you were taught to count?" "Why?" he or she asks. "Because that's the way the person designed the picture to be completed when all the black dots are connected. When you connect them in the correct order, you will then be able to see a complete picture." Putting a hand in mine, I helped connect the numbered dots. "Now I see the picture; now I understand!" It's a key!

Think about the numbered dots in your production process. Is there a continuous line of activities until the product or service is completed? Can you see the picture, the flow of the materials through your shop floor

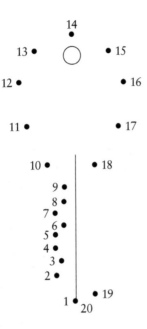

or office? Or does it flow erratically all over the place, like a pile of snarled fish line?

Connecting the dots for a process can illuminate a situation as no other method can. It makes your work process come alive, making it easy to study and see needed change and improvement. It's also the first step toward establishing a standard procedure, an integral part of any quality improvement effort.

Processes can be simple or complex and accomplish the same task. The key is to establish a process that leaves no room for error, yet is easy to follow. When documenting your process flow, be sure the floor layout matches it.

When a process is visible to the eye, you will benefit from a more efficient, collaborative effort to preventing errors. Analyze the *process* when errors occur, not the person performing the process.

PROCESS FLOW VS. FLOOR LAYOUT

Comparing a task flow diagram with an actual floor layout to determine inefficiencies within a process applies equally to administration, service, and product areas. When analyzing a hybrid circuit manufacturing process, we used the mapping technique shown in Figure 7.6. I discovered that the product flow was not compatible with the work space or machine layout. This resulted in many conflicts among the 20 or so people involved in producing the product. In addition, using a pedometer, I found that each person walked an average of 2.2 miles while processing one set of components. When I asked why the process was laid out the way it was, I discovered that management didn't want to spend money to move an AC power bus! In effect, the cost of the power bus relocation was paid many times over because of the wasted time and effort.

The product was in transit a disproportionate amount of time compared to actual processing time. (When questioned, however, workers said they actually liked the arrangement because they got a lot of exercise!) The bottom line was that this company paid for a lot of non–value-adding activity, cutting directly into profits. Eventually the floor layout was matched to the process tasks, and processing time was reduced more than 50 percent, with a corresponding decrease in inventory.

During a two-day Continuous Improvement in Daily Work workshop conducted for a law office, existing work flows were mapped and participants discovered that their desks and office furniture were not arranged in the best way. After reviewing their documented process flow (see Figure 7.7), they rearranged things and were able to report the next day that efficiency and communications had immediately improved. Instant improvement results are frequently possible when processes are properly documented, analyzed, and changed.

When processes are flowcharted, certain elements are often left out.

- No times associated with flow (does the action take minutes, hours, days?)

- No indication of why something is happening (actions can easily be left out)

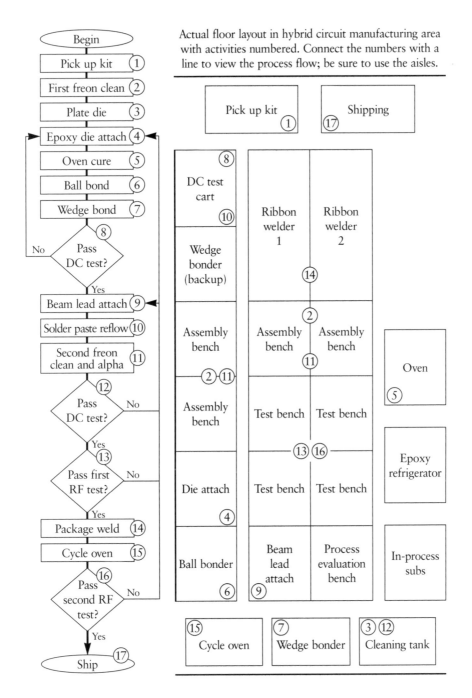

Figure 7.6. High-level hybrid component process and actual floor layout.

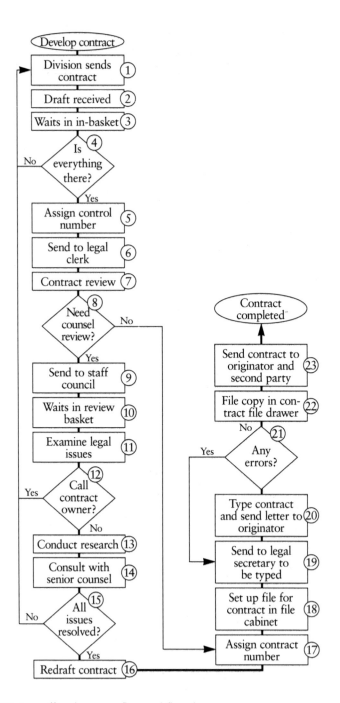

Figure 7.7. Law office document flow and floor layout.

Actual floor layout in law office with numbered events. Connect the numbers with a line to view the process flow; be sure to use the aisles.

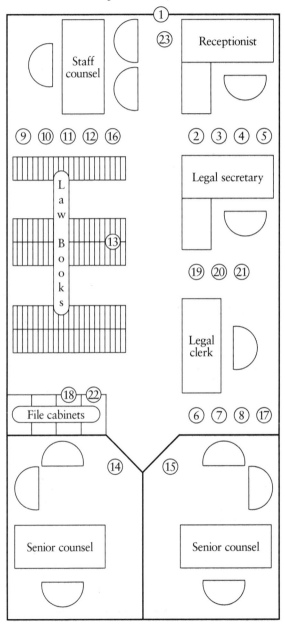

Figure 7.7. *Continued.*

- No relative scale of action items (too much detail in some, not enough in others)

- No responsibility assigned to tasks (who will get things done?)

- Date updated and effective (any sense of urgency or timeliness will be lost)

Remember that documenting processes is initially aimed at trying to find new ways to use existing resources such as people, tools, and equipment. The goal is to use brainpower to find improvements without extra cost.

Improvement can be targeted in four categories: materials, methods (processes), machine (equipment), and manpower (men and women's labor). When looking for labor improvements, you must provide the latitude for employees to experiment and tinker with their tools, equipment, and procedures to find better ways to do the work. They need to understand the concepts of *self-check*—inspecting your own work while you perform it, and *successive check*—inspection in a cross-trained situation where two people know the same job and the second person inspects subconsciously. This occurs naturally and often when cross-functional processes are understood.

———————————— ■ ■ ■ ————————————

A common example of self-check is a computer spell-checking algorithm that assists writers in finding and correcting spelling or grammar errors. A successive check example in this same area would be an editor checking a writer's work. Both checks can ultimately become an integral part of the process, leading to fail-safe protection that prevents errors from ever occurring.

———————————— ■ ■ ■ ————————————

When first documenting your own work process, record the process exactly as you are currently doing it; don't try to improve it as you map it. This will provide a good record of where you were so that you will be able to see how the changes being made will eventually pay off.

Remember that many small, incremental steps will be much more beneficial than trying to make large changes all at once. This may be hard to grasp initially because we have always rewarded the home-run hitter—the star—and not the person that gets a single or a bunt. However, change in businesses and organizations is more easily implemented and controlled when accomplished as continual, small-step process improvements.

The comparison of old and improved process flows in Figure 7.8 illustrates how engineers improved their project management process. In the original (old) process shown, the information was never stabilized throughout a project. Also, notice the activity block in the first example that goes nowhere. The improved process flow shows items in a refined, more correct sequence, simplifying the entire process. Notice too how the information is properly gathered.

GATHERING DATA AND FACTS

Before making any procedural or process changes, we suggest gathering enough process information (use a check sheet or a visual map of the flow) to support your change efforts. Data should be gathered with the idea of taking action—to determine where to focus your energy, verify a process procedure's steps, verify that a problem exists, measure its magnitude or size, and understand its nature.

Gathering data is the first step toward innovation and the removal of non–value-adding activities. Data and facts are needed to implement innovation into a process and stimulate the need to do something. Without observing what is happening, people tend to take the attitude that "no news is good news" and do nothing. Gathering process data stimulates action. When a process is working fine, there is no impetus to analyze it for improvement. Collecting data about the process will reverse this tendency and encourage people to look for small-step improvements. Remember that you don't need to have a problem to make things better.

The objective is to establish a method of examining processes that will help you accumulate data relating to them. The data must be honest and accurate if improvements are to be made. Methods of data collection can

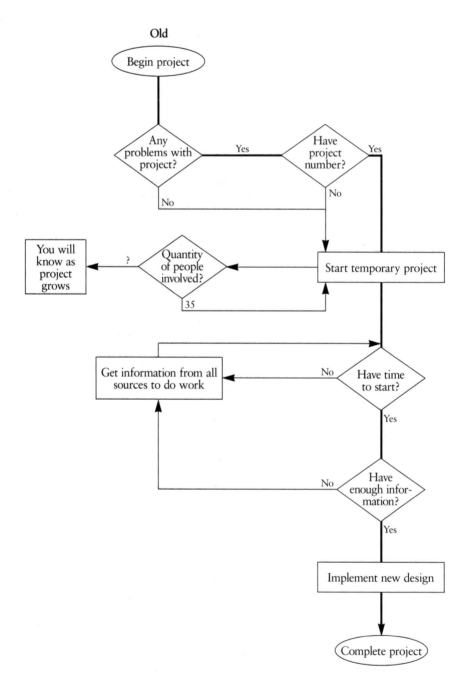

Figure 7.8. Project engineers' old and improved planning process.

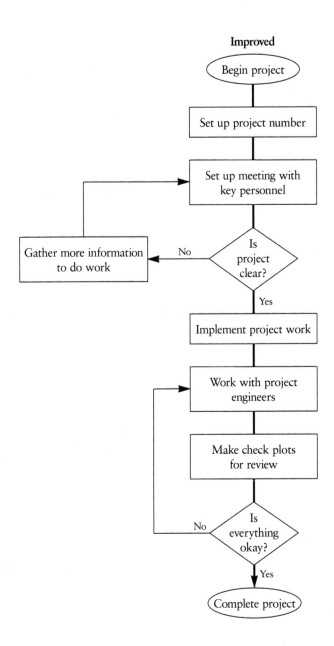

Figure 7.8. *Continued.*

include check sheets, process flow maps, activity-based costing, questionnaires, sample tests, library research, interviews, pictures/photographs, a camcorder, computer database searches, benchmarking, and so on.

I have observed that whatever is measured usually has a tendency to be improved. Without measures, nothing happens. Your goal is to track the accomplishments of a particular task: What is happening? Are you getting better? Are you reaching set goals?

To present data and facts as useful information, use visual aids—charts and graphs—to make it easy for everyone to understand. Pie charts, bar charts, line graphs, paired bar charts, and the like all help to show trends and make data easy to interpret and act on (be sure to label them). Employees have a responsibility to respond immediately to gathered data, suggestions for improvement, or uncovered problems. Management can support the effort by empowering people to stop and fix things, improve the process now, and get to the root cause so the same situation will not occur again. Fix things permanently; temporary fixes usually have to be fixed again.

ADDRESSING ADMINISTRATION AND SERVICE AREAS

I often conduct a workshop titled Visual Methods for Improving Process Performance (an SPC workshop with limited mathematics). Few, if any, administration and service personnel attended the workshops, while manufacturing personnel were in abundance. Since the majority of employees in companies work in administration and services, an opportunity to address this audience was observed. After many discussions with administrative and service managers of these areas, I designed a pilot workshop during my evenings and weekends. (Details of the workshop are explained in chapter 9.) It was aimed at all types of employees regardless of where they worked (administration, services, and manufacturing groups). The first workshop was presented to a VP of administration's staff and approved, then an endless stream of employees were sent to scheduled workshops. Post-workshop surveys of participants indicated that the workshop was very beneficial and that people wanted to know more. Demand became so great that workshop logistics became a problem.

PRACTICING WHAT I PREACH

When presenting workshops on an everyday basis, little things were constantly falling through the cracks. One day I'd forget name tents; another time I'd overschedule myself. Mentally I changed many things, but I still continued to forget things during workshop preparations. "Take time to analyze the process you've used," I told myself.

My change process began with charting today's flow of the steps used in preparation and presentation of the workshop, identifying what was currently occurring (see Figure 7.9).

The first step: Promote, make potential participants aware of the workshop. This was accomplished using three methods: (1) making presentations to members of the Corporate Quality Council, representing all areas of the company; (2) advertising in the company newsletter, the Portland Community College catalog (located on the Tektronix campus), and the company's electronic mail system; and (3) calling various financial managers and presenting overviews to their staffs.

The next step involved receiving lists of participants from group managers. Once a list of participants was received (an effort was made to train customer and supplier groups together, if possible), I made sure my presentation materials were current and updated. I removed any discussion marks made during the previous presentation. Name tent cards were printed as notices were mailed to workshop participants.

On the day of the workshop, a room was set up for group training; materials and name cards were placed on tables. The workshop was presented according to its outline, and an evaluation was completed by each participant before leaving the workshop. Suggestions for improvement were welcomed, and improvements were often made.

Six weeks later, a notice was sent to all participants regarding the scheduled review meeting to share results. Overheads were presented by participants on how they applied the techniques learned in the workshop.

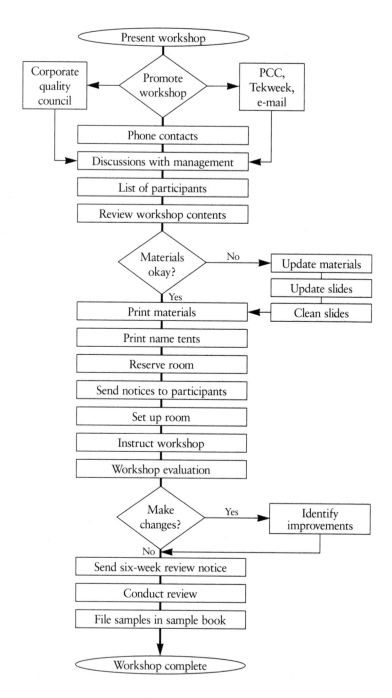

Figure 7.9. Preparation before workshop presentation.

Everyone listened, discussed, shared, and learned what others were doing in their daily work activities. Samples of shared process flows were then filed in a sample book.

The documented flow did not solve my logistics problem. Are the steps in the right sequence? Is the process due for reengineering? The process was rethought and streamlined. Instead of preparing the materials before each workshop, preparation was moved to after each workshop. Only one review was now required instead of two. Preparing table name tent cards was determined to be a wasted step; the tent cards were left blank so that workshop participants could write their own names on them (rarely did they sit where I had put their name cards). The process was getting simpler.

Logistics problems still prevailed. After three process reviews, my problems were eliminated (see Figure 7.10).

1. When a room was reserved, I entered it on my personal calendar at the same time. Often I had failed to do this and had over-booked.

2. Materials were now printed before sending out notices to the next workshop participants.

3. Review notices were no longer sent to remind participants. They were reminded at the end of each workshop with an overhead displaying the planned review date.

4. The review time was moved from six weeks to one week. It was found that very few participants were doing anything until the last week of the six weeks. Management would now see results faster.

5. We now prepared a sample book, so that others could observe the activities of their customers or suppliers.

6. A check sheet of activities displayed on the improved process flow map was made, and my logistic problems disappeared.

I tried these process flow techniques at home. After watching my wife prepare breakfast for several mornings, I noticed that she made lots of trips to the refrigerator, sink, and table. I suggested that she carry more

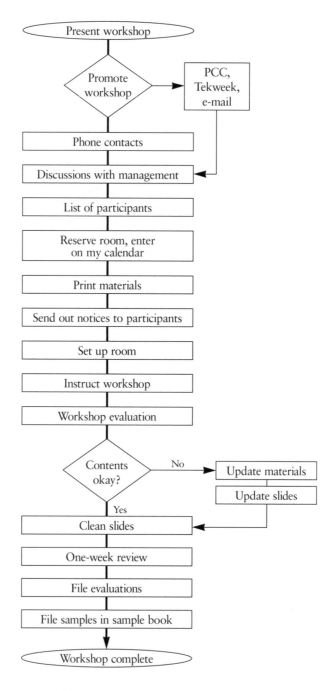

Figure 7.10. Preparation after workshop presentation.

than one item at a time. Did the breakfast routine improve? Yes, I now have to prepare my own breakfast in eight minutes. She used to do it in 20 minutes; now she sleeps in a little longer.

ANOTHER FOCUSING TOOL: THE PARETO CONCEPT

The main purpose of a Pareto chart is to *prioritize data and focus people's attention*. The Pareto principle as applied to problems says that: "if you work on 20 percent of the problems, you will get an 80 percent impact, while working on the remaining 80 percent of the problems will give only a 20 percent impact."

While it is tempting to use this tool to find out where to invest money, we suggest that everyone use the Pareto principle to look at the largest occurrence of *events*, rather than the largest dollar items. If a process problem is being looked at and solved over and over, hidden costs associated with the effort often go unnoticed and undocumented. Many times visible dollars tied to a particular function or item catch a manager's or supervisor's eye. The problem may have happened only once but the tendency is to "save that $500." In reality, another item with 50 occurrences costs $15 each, plus the hidden costs involved with reworking the problem (a $750 savings).

Pareto charting is very useful when addressing problems occurring within a work process. Its visual nature helps you focus on the largest problems that need solutions.

HOW TO CONSTRUCT A PARETO CHART

Making a Pareto chart is not difficult once you have categorized and tabulated frequency-of-occurrence data in the form of a check sheet. Make sure all the data are from the same time period—hour, day, week, month, quarter, or year. Begin with a picture frame.

Framework. Draw the overall frame first. Label the bottom horizontal axis *categories*, the left vertical axis *occurrences*, and the right vertical axis *percentage of return.* The height of the vertical axis is determined by the sum of all the category bars. The total number of occurrences identified on your check sheet should be labeled at the top of the left vertical axis. The right vertical axis should be equal in height to the left vertical axis and show percentage from zero to 100 percent (see Figure 7.11).

Category Bars, Left and Right Vertical Axis. The number of category bars should be equally spaced on the horizontal axis. You will have to determine how many categories you want to consider by looking at the data on your check sheet. For instance, you may want to lump the many small occurrences into one specific category titled *Other,* or you may want to list them all separately, depending on the categories. The

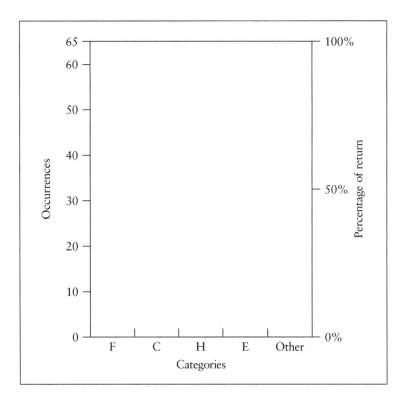

Figure 7.11. Constructing the frame.

right-most category column labeled *Other* is where any lumped categories are placed, and may not be the smallest in descending order. That's okay. Plot the remaining occurrences vertically in descending order from left to right, using the data from your check sheet (see Figure 7.12). Remember that the Pareto chart is a focusing tool—you cannot address everything at once.

Cumulative Curve. Once all the categories are plotted, draw a cumulative curve starting at the lower left vertex and continuing up through all the categories, where the curve should end at the upper right vertex. This is accomplished by stacking one category quantity on top of another on the left axis and drawing an intersecting line up from the right corner of each

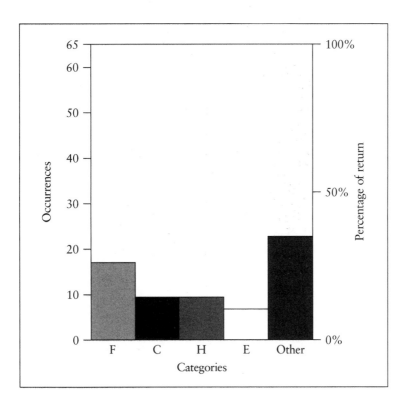

Figure 7.12. Entering the category bars.

category bar and making a dot. After all the dots have been established, connect them with lines. This becomes the cumulative curve (see Figure 7.13). Hopefully, the curve will end at the upper vertex. If it exceeds or is under the vertex, something is wrong with your chart. Review the data and construction process and redo the chart.

The cumulative curve tells you two things: (1) all data have been included properly if it ends in the upper right hand corner, and (2) the percentage of return that can be expected if the root cause of a problem is removed is demonstrated. Percentage of return is found by sighting across the chart from each dot to the right vertical axis. If category F is removed, 18 percent of the problems will be removed. If categories F and C are removed, 28 percent of the problems will be removed. Remember

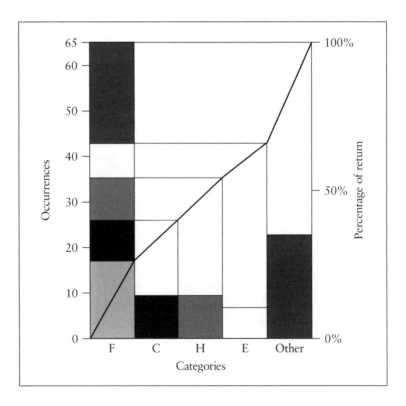

Figure 7.13. Adding the cumulative line.

that all data displayed should be of the same time period, or the data will be skewed.

Interpreting the Results. The largest type of occurrence on the left side of the chart provides the first indication of what to work on (see Figure 7.14). Percentage of return for any category of occurrence can be found by looking along the top of the category bar to the right axis to see what the reduction will be when the root cause of the problem is removed.

Some other construction hints include the following: Make the chart large enough to see when posted on a wall and as simple as possible to encourage people to study it. Make sure you include a title at the top that

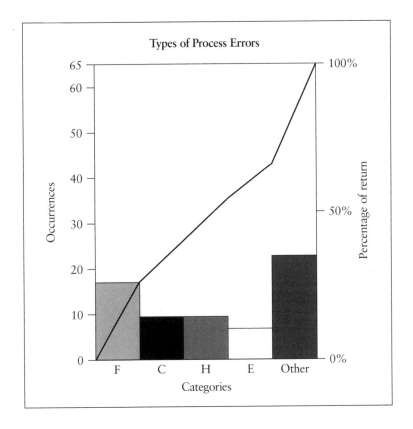

Figure 7.14. Completed Pareto chart.

clearly defines what the chart shows and whether it relates to other charts. Include a legend with all relevant data, including symbols, and label all items clearly and accurately. The Pareto charting method can be used to further break down a single category, if required.

If managers and employees are faced with using their companies' resources wisely, the Pareto chart will aid them. As you can see, the Pareto chart serves to separate the vital few problems from the trivial many. The vital few are often selected as improvement projects. The trivial many (*other* category) only rarely become projects. It's not that they *shouldn't* become projects; but they only affect specific individuals, and therefore specific individuals must often attack these problems on their own.

CHAPTER 8

MEASUREMENTS AND FEEDBACK

AIM OF THIS CHAPTER

The aim of this chapter is to provide a vision of new measures, their applications, and their correlations. My philosophy is to measure: If you don't measure it, you cannot control it or improve it. Many traditional measures no longer apply with improved structures and processing methods. If leadership wants the business to grow or maintain momentum, it must make changes in its measurement systems. Without changing your existing measures, you may not be keeping a very accurate score or you won't know if you are lagging behind, maintaining, or moving ahead. Make your measurements visible to everyone in the workforce.

Along with traditional measures, businesses and organizations should combine customer satisfaction, internal business processes, learning, and financial results to reshape their organizations. Because TQM offers no qualitative measures, cost drivers—factors that determine the final cost of an operation—will change your business.

HIGH-SPEED OPERATIONS LEAD TO PROFITS

Businesses are driven by a perpetual sense of time. First the time clock created artificial time pressures. (Remember time management studies?)

Now we have teleconferencing, fax machines, Internet software, voice mail, e-mail, overnight mail, mobile phones, jet planes, and computer technology based on the nanosecond with response times in increments of one-billionth of a second.

In business, *optimizing order-to-delivery response time is the best way to gain a competitive edge.* Under old paradigms for success, the race was won by the business that provided customized products or services whenever it promised or delivered them. In today's fast-paced competitive world, the business with the quickest order-to-delivery response time wins the sale. This is true especially if your competitors' products or services are comparable to your own in price and quality. Recognizing the value of a quick response time can achieve astonishing and powerful results even if a company's product or service is not appreciably different from that of competitors. Quick response time yields speed and flexibility for which many companies are willing to pay a premium. Total process speed (velocity) then becomes essential to ensure shorter promised deliveries.

Improving process speed or order-to-delivery approaches could prove an awesome but necessary challenge to every business in this time-competitive decade. Time-based or order-to-delivery strategies force the rethinking or reengineering of operations. You may have the best product or service in the world, but that doesn't matter if you can't get it to customers quickly. It's not the big businesses that crush the little businesses; the quick ones crush the slow ones. Total supply-chain management, the integration of all process activities, becomes necessary. If there's one broken link in the chain, you have a major problem.

■ ■ ■

When Philip B. Crosby, author of the book *Quality Is Free* (1979), made his controversial statement, he meant that if you improve the quality of products or services, you ultimately save time and money. Thus, the actual cost of quality decreases, with a corresponding improvement in customer response time.

■ ■ ■

Time, as Albert Einstein pointed out, is relative. Establish a goal of becoming two to three times faster in your responses to customers. Create stretch goals that will necessitate process rethinking or reengineering by operational people to be more responsive. People must know that they can't do the same daily tasks in the same way and become this much faster. You must be willing to move your workers out of their comfort zone. During your rethinking or reengineering efforts, you must constantly stay in touch with your customers. Customer satisfaction can be associated with faster payment of invoices. With the speed of technology changes, constantly focusing on the customer helps you prioritize improvements. Once you know who is and who can be a valuable customer to your business, invest your energy and resources in improving process speed to satisfying them. Time is money; saving it is up to you.

I am often asked, "What's causing excessive order-to-delivery response times in most businesses?" I've often observed that as much as 95 percent of processing time consists of waiting: waiting for sales orders to be processed; waiting for credit reports; waiting for engineering documentation; waiting for a process to be corrected; waiting for supplies; waiting in various bottleneck areas—waiting, waiting, waiting! All this waiting stretches the order-to-delivery total throughput time. To break the vicious cycle, you must often review and then reengineer the entire supply chain. Balance and flow must be obtained to eliminate bottlenecks, and non–value-adding activities must be removed from all areas of the process.

In 1979, I attended a presentation at Tektronix by George Stalk, a consultant with The Boston Consulting Group, just after his return from spending several years in Japan studying processing practices. Listening to him woke me up. He presented example after example of his findings in Japan. Whenever Japanese businesses cut their time to produce an item, profits automatically went up. This in itself was not so surprising, but how they reduced processing times and limited parts usage was. Many companies, he stated, were employing hoshin kanri—the merging of strategic visions/missions, goals, and objectives with production management and control—to reduce their process total throughput times. Every company using hoshin planning was enjoying reduced total throughput times.

In general, Japanese businesses focus heavily on time management and consistently produce products and provide services at a cheaper rate than most U.S. companies do. The end result or output may be the same, but U.S. processing costs are higher and profits lower—to a large degree, because so many non–value-adding activities are inflicted on our processes.

Many U.S. companies have not yet learned that *simplifying each and every activity within a process* will result in increased profits. Notice that we are talking about processes again. George Stalk observed that *time-based* companies focusing on improving their processes' total through-put time grow on the average three times faster and show two times more profit than *results-based* companies that focus only on bottom-line dollars. Whatever the product or service is, it must move expediently. Process speed (velocity) creates a whole new world of opportunities. Inventories shrink, write-offs are smaller and less frequent, fewer people are required, money is released from your line of credit, and interest costs drop dramatically. Your competitiveness is enhanced, and profit margins grow.

Time consumption is quantifiable; it can be measured and managed. Opportunities to compress time can be quite radical. You can shrink manufacturing processes from 110 days to three days and end-of-month book closings in accounting from 28 days to two days. Reduced processing times like these can occur when you start to

- Structure work flows and processes in a horizontal mode.
- Enable daily work to be done in a parallel, side-by-side fashion.
- Compress the response time in everything you do.

Often people in manufacturing have said, "We can always salvage wasted materials" (to make up for poor, inefficient materials or processes). But time is not like materials. There is no waste salvage in time. Once time is lost, it is gone forever. You must learn to do right things right the first time, every time. There are two parts to this principle: *The right thing* addresses how you do what you do, and *the first time* addresses the question of how well you do it.

TIME IS MONEY

In 1748, Benjamin Franklin wrote in his *Advice to Young Tradesmen* that "time is money." Time has a strategic value, and nobody wants to pay for extra costs incurred from a slow process. Today, cutting-edge companies are focusing on time-based management techniques as a critical competitive advantage. They treat time in the same way as expenses and inventory. The result is reduced costs and more sophisticated products and services.

Older, cost-based strategies required management to drive down expenses, usually at the cost of responsiveness. New, time-based strategies facilitate rapid response to attract customers and increase innovation by concentrating on the elimination of timely process delays: queue times, excessive transportation, inspection, and rework. This means virtually *no* non–value-adding activities. A productive system means lower cost for customers.

Time consumption is something management seldom monitors. Yet time is a more competitive measure than financial measurements. Time is money. You must reduce total throughput times.

Reducing response times through time-based (supply-chain management) strategies usually results in competitors not knowing how to compete against you. Time consumption is common in everything you (or your competitors) do. Customers increasingly ask for faster deliveries of quality products or services. A service part that arrives in one week instead of one day could create a lack of satisfaction in the customer's mind. Every process offers an opportunity for a study to improve speed (decrease its total throughput time). With process speed (velocity or total throughput time) comes dollar savings and competitive advantage because quick delivery response time captures business. If you stand still in today's global market environment, competition will drive you out of business. You may have the best product or service in the world, but it doesn't matter if you can't get it to your customers quickly. Process speed and delivery speed create superior competitive weapons. Look what UPS has done.

MBWA: MANAGEMENT BY WALKING AROUND

Management can observe processes and assist in decreasing total throughput time. When managers use MBWA as one of their internal communication tools, they must be sure that if they ask a question on the floor, they are prepared to wait around and listen to the answer. When time is not taken to pause long enough at any one spot, a wrong answer may be received. There are several good questions for managers to ask operational personnel: "Is there anything you would like to see improved in the process you work in? In the material or services you receive?" "How would you reduce costs?" When an answer is given, ask the person if he or she would like to participate on a learning team to address the issue. Other questions might be about how quality is defined within their job title and function and how it is measured.

Associates will do whatever management asks them to do. If managers wants backorders reduced, employees reduce backorders. If they want more orders shipped on time, associates do whatever is necessary to ship on time. When they decree a slash in inventory to cut costs, sure enough, inventory will go down. If management wants an improvement in total head count productivity, head count is reduced to achieve it. Notice how these typical management goals focus only on results criteria. Management traditionally focuses on results because that's what stockholders want to see improved. Management must begin including process criteria in its periodic measures.

RESULTS VS. PROCESS CRITERIA

There are three fundamental ways to measure performance: results criteria, process criteria, and the two together. A common mistake business management makes today is to focus only on the short-term weekly, monthly or quarterly measures, which inevitably means focusing on results criteria. Are sales where they should be? Are costs of doing business where they should be? Are profits where they should be? When looking at these criteria, it is easy to blame people who perform the process instead of the process itself. After all, people are doing the work; they must be responsible for the results. In fact, it is usually not the people at all, but the processes, that are not adequately producing what they should be. If the focus is only on results criteria, seldom will you be able to make the changes or improvements necessary for long-term business success.

Results criteria focus on traditional performance measures such as quantities produced, delivery times, cycle times, shipping dates, bill-of-material accuracy, inventory turns, financial results, expenses, earnings, sales, sales per person, and so on.

Process criteria focus on establishing common procedures, the discipline to follow them, and new performance measures such as total throughput time, activity-based costing, defects per unit, inputs from suppliers, outputs to customers, direct customer feedback and communications, innovation, involvement, and empowerment. These criteria are described as follows:

Common Procedures and Discipline. Common procedures to accomplish similar tasks are mandatory for productivity improvement. If more than one person, group, or division is accomplishing the same task or function, they each should be doing it in the same manner. Unfortunately, many businesses and organizations do not have common procedures in place. This is frequently the result of a lack of discipline.

■ ■ ■

Eight different divisions at a large electronics manufacturing company were using their own specific paperwork to send items to a central distribution point, where the receiving department had to adapt to eight different shipping forms and eight different labels on the packages. The information contained in the forms and labels was essentially the same, but eight different processes were required to deal with them. When management changed the mind-set of distribution center personnel to focus on the divisions as their suppliers, center personnel went to the divisions and provided data supporting the benefits of a common document being used by all. With assistance from the eight divisions, the distribution center (the customer) created a single form, streamlining the total process and saving the company money.

■ ■ ■

Auditing (measuring the accuracy of) a procedure for a given process is not rocket science. We recommend the following:

1. Obtain a master copy of the process procedure documentation (and its supporting bill of material for manufactured products).

2. Follow the process flow currently in use. Highlight any discrepancies found in the sequence of steps or the quantities used on the procedure documentation. Do not mention any discrepancies identified at this time to the operators.

3. (Manufacturing only) After completing the procedures audit on the floor, audit the bill-of-material quantities against highlighted quantities on the procedure.

4. Bring common operators together and discuss what was found. Ask the operators to establish and agree on a common process method.

5. Prepare a closed-loop corrective action report (engineering change notice) for action to take place.

Total Throughput Time. Throughput in a process is usually thought of in two ways: department or function time, and total throughput time. *Department or function time* is the time from when a task is started until it is completed in one function, group, or department. *Total throughput time* (TTT) is broader, being a measure of the actual time from the beginning of all cross-functional, interdepartmental, horizontal activities until all supplier activities have been completed for one item.

The TTT measure is recommended over single departmental or functional time because it relates to the total process. When TTT has been considered and optimized in all cross-functional workplaces, evidence has consistently shown that quality goes up, the cost of doing business goes down, a greater variety of products and services can be offered, and customer response or delivery time becomes shorter.

The ultimate goal of measuring TTT is to improve customer response time, whether you are introducing or producing a product or providing a service. Make it a key competitive weapon for the future.

TTT indicates how long it takes to produce a product or service from the beginning to the end of the total process, as opposed to traditional cycle time, which is a measure of only how frequently a product or service comes out of the end of the process. If you simply measure how quickly people do things in an attempt to speed them up, they will go into a hurry mode and probably increase the defect rate in direct proportion to their increased speed. TTT is the correct quality measure to use when trying to increase process speed and response time. Reward people for doing things more quickly through an improved process, not for doing the same job using the same process for 25 years in a row.

TTT will enable you to "know the time and keep score" for all processes (administrative, service, and product groups). This measure provides the best data available to help you meet the goals of quick customer response and defect-free processes. Establishing and meeting TTT goals cannot be emphasized enough and, once it is understood by all employees, it will result in huge benefits to your company. All work becomes simplified when no problems are passed downstream to the next part of the process or activity. Quick response to customers, internal or external, leads directly to increased profits.

A large part of what most people do during their daily work tasks today is related to correcting, fixing, and solving problems created upstream of their activity. None of this work adds any value to the end product or service, and in fact adds cost to the process. This waste can be eliminated by employing TTT and activity-based costing measures.

There are two areas to focus on when measuring throughput time in your business: visible inventory and invisible inventory. *Visible inventory* includes any type of raw material, product, data, or information used to produce something that is visible to the eye. Items are purchased or received, labor is performed on those items adding value to it, the item then moves for more labor to be performed on it (adding more value), and finally the finished product is shipped. As Figure 8.1 shows, labor and materials are continually added over time, increasing the cost of the item. There are often non–value-adding steps in the process— the resting of dollars invested during a process that need to be removed.

Invisible inventory includes any support function characteristic of service groups—marketing, engineering, administration, sales, distribution, finance, information systems, and so on—that are not visible to the eye. It is just as real, in terms of cost, as physical (visible) inventory, but is rarely focused on because what happens is often not seen.

Figure 8.1 shows how a business administration and services, materials, and labor are added over time (cost) with value being continually added (more cost) to produce a product or service. Time is required (TTT) until

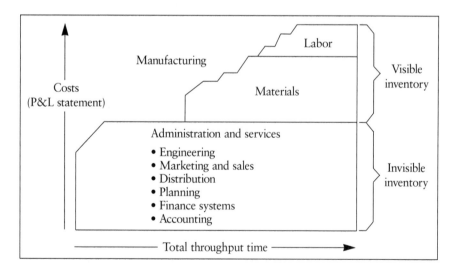

Figure 8.1. Cost vs. time profile of total business organization.

all activities are completed. Most manufacturing organizations have been working to reduce expenses and improve operations over the last decade. However, as you can see in Figure 8.1, there is much to be gained by focusing on administration and service activities (overhead).

I have observed many companies doing a good job of simplifying manufacturing processes with SPC, TQC, and JIT (demand pull), but most have done a poor job transforming administration and service area processes. Ironically, the same non–value-adding steps need to be reduced or eliminated in these areas to improve productivity: removing inspection, rework, transportation, storage, and other non–value-adding activities. If you look only at your profit-and-loss statement (materials and labor) you will not see the overhead costs, even though in developed countries, two-thirds to three-fourths of employment, output, and costs are in administration and service areas.

MEASURING TOTAL THROUGHPUT TIME

By following five broad steps, you can accurately determine the total throughput time for any function in your business. These steps have been discussed in detail in previous chapters and are presented here as an overall procedure.

1. Document your processes.

    —Include all decisions, choices made, and actions taken.

    —Label all activities for tracking purposes.

2. Measure (at least three times) the actual time required to perform each complete, real-life function, then use the smallest time as your standard.

3. Track several items through the process to see if the same procedure occurs over and over or if different processes are being used.

4. Circle the process steps that take the longest, then break them down into smaller increments to reduce their time.

5. Challenge the longest times by using activity-based costing drivers.

MEASURING THROUGHPUT TIME EXAMPLE: DELI CONTRACT

A contract was received to help reduce the long wait times and eliminate counter confusion at a local deli operation. This particular deli, it seemed, always had customers lined up waiting for service, waiting to place orders, waiting for orders to be delivered, and waiting to pay. "How can I help you, Boss?" the counter person would ask. Orders were listened to, but seldom written down. Yelling an order to the food preparer was a common practice. Most customers ordered a beverage to go with their food. Once the food or drink was ready, it was put on a waiting counter. The counter person would pick up the beverage and food before entering it in the cash register. Many times the beverage and food orders did not match and would have to be reordered. The front counter personnel again yelled to the food preparers to prepare it: "I need a Greek burger, pronto!"

Customer orders were spoken as they were placed in a bag (quality check) and entered into the cash register. After tallying the cash register, the total was quoted to the customer. Money was received from the customer, change handed back, and the cash register closed. If a problem was observed during the process, rework steps began immediately. To eliminate the confusion, the following four process review steps were taken.

1. *Document today's process.* The deli operation's total process flow was documented with the front counter and food preparer's assistance. The total process included 20 high-level process steps (see Figure 8.2).

2. *Gather average performance times.* Process times were gathered for all 20 activities on the documented process in 1. Each time was written on the chart beside the appropriate numeric (see Figure 8.3). To arrive at an average time, each activity was measured with a stopwatch a minimum of three times.

3. *Identify process flows.* Several process flows were identified while physically tracking orders as they were processed (all scenarios will not be discussed in this example). Total throughput times

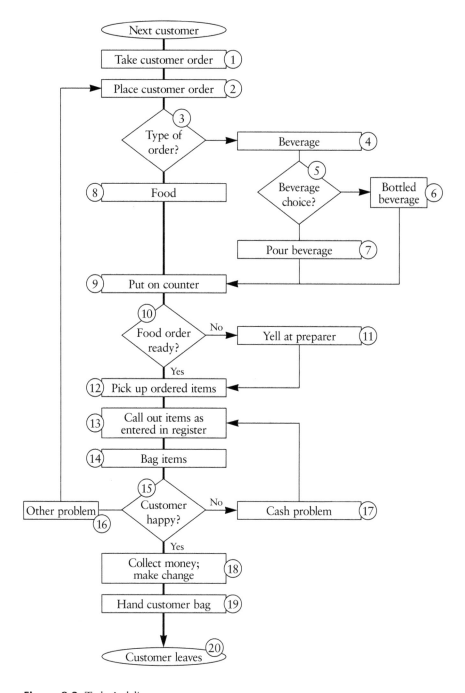

Figure 8.2. Today's deli process.

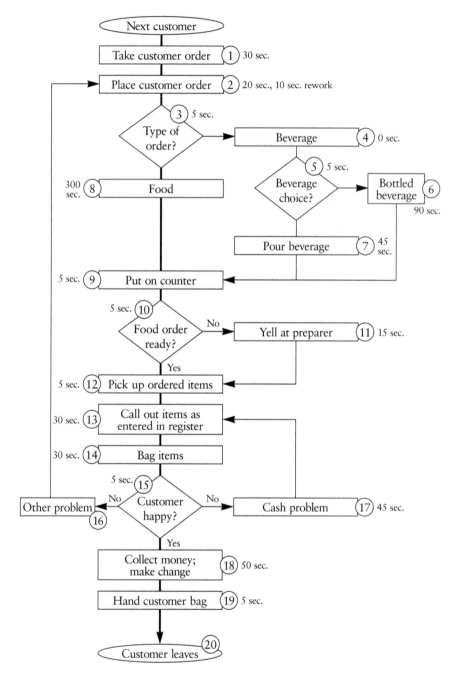

Figure 8.3. Today's deli process, with average times for events.

were calculated for (1) food and drink order; (2) food and bottled beverage order; and (3) food and drink order, with a wrong drink presented to the customer (see Figure 8.4). The food and drink throughput time involved 14 steps and took a total of 580 seconds to process; the food and bottled beverage time involved 14 process steps and 625 seconds to process; and the food and drink order with a rework drink involved 19 process steps and 660 seconds to process. Rework added 35 additional seconds of time. The food and drink process was found to be the most common process. Knowing that throughput times were too long, a decision was made to benchmark a typical fast food restaurant's service. The question was, what is a good throughput time?

Food and drink order		Food and bottled beverage		Food and drink, with drink rework	
1	30 seconds	1	30 seconds	1	30 seconds
2	20 seconds	2	20 seconds	2	20 seconds
3	5 seconds	3	5 seconds	3	5 seconds
5	5 seconds	5	5 seconds	5	5 seconds
7	45 seconds	6	90 seconds	7	45 seconds
8	300 seconds	8	300 seconds	8	300 seconds
9	5 seconds	9	5 seconds	9	5 seconds
10	5 seconds	10	5 seconds	10	5 seconds
12	5 seconds	12	5 seconds	12	5 seconds
13	30 seconds	13	30 seconds	13	30 seconds
14	30 seconds	14	30 seconds	14	30 seconds
15	5 seconds	15	5 seconds	15	5 seconds
18	50 seconds	18	50 seconds	16	45 seconds
19	5 seconds	19	5 seconds	2	10 seconds
				3	5 seconds
				5	5 seconds
				7	45 seconds
				18	50 seconds
				19	5 seconds
580 seconds		625 seconds		660 seconds	

Figure 8.4. Total throughput times for different observed processes.

4. *Redesign the process.* A new, state-of-the-art fast food restaurant was visited and its process visually observed and documented, with several orders followed and timed. The deli's processes were then compared with those of the fast food restaurant. The total time for the fast food restaurant's process similar to the one at the deli contained a total throughput of 14 steps and 375 seconds of time, versus 580 seconds for the deli. A savings of 205 seconds, or 3.25 minutes per order, was achieved by the restaurant.

The servicing process for the deli was changed to match that of the restaurant. This resulted in a minimum of two short queues, rather then three long ones. Other dramatic changes were implemented.

- The total process was reengineered (see Figure 8.5). Compare Figures 8.2 and 8.5. The deli's process could not have had such a large throughput time reduction if this had not been done.

- Compare where the cash register is placed in step 13 of Figure 8.2; the deli's redesigned process is in step 1. In the deli's redesigned flow process it is now the first step, not the thirteenth. This eliminates orders from being taken wrong. Rework or reordering is now almost nonexistent. Most rework today is related to customers who change their mind, not to the work performed by the deli's personnel.

- Notice that the cost of serving the beverage was shifted to the customer. The customer was told, "You can have all the beverage refills you would like." It is cheaper to do this, rather than using personnel to fill the cups. Note that most customers still order large cups to fill (at more profit) rather than filling the smaller cup several times.

ANOTHER WAY

At an Association for Manufacturing Excellence conference in Wisconsin in 1989, another method was observed for measuring a customer order process to identify improvement areas. A very high-level process map was presented to the audience (see Figure 8.6). The project leader then asked the audience, "Where do you think we should be focusing our time to

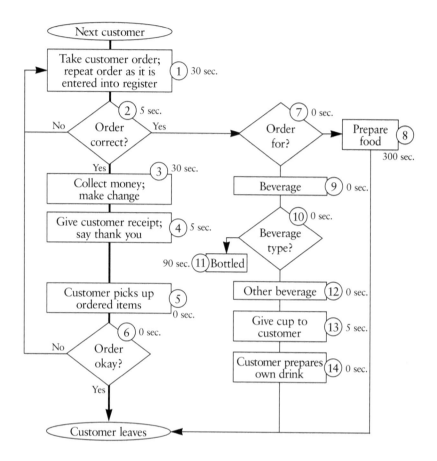

Figure 8.5. Redesigned deli process.

reduce our customer order throughput time?" She asked for a raise of hands as she pointed to each activity block, then made check marks behind the blocks identifying various activities. The majority of those in the audience identified production of the item as their choice, gut feeling.

Next, she displayed actual throughput time data in the form of bars representing time for each activity (see Figure 8.7). It was easy to see that the step requiring the most time was accounts receivable (gut feelings were not correct). This item, however, would not be attacked, because it would require giving discounts for early payment. The next longest time

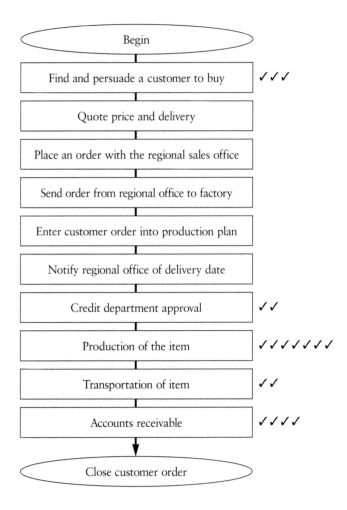

Figure 8.6. High-level flowchart with checks.

occurred during the process step quoting price and delivery. This, she said, "they did something about!" She then discussed how a computer and modem in a briefcase and a customer's telephone were used to interface with a production scheduler in the factory to shrink waiting time. Implementation of the team's ideas dramatically reduced the time for committing orders from 12 days to 10 minutes. Visually looking at detailed process data helps identify improvement areas quickly.

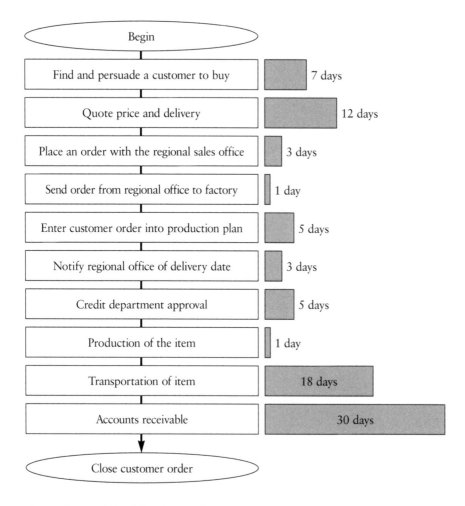

Figure 8.7. High-level flowchart with time bars.

Activity-based costing is the gathering of cost information, breaking down and calculating the cost of each process step into little batches—cost drivers, the factors that determine the final cost of an operation. Once a process map has actual throughput time associated with its activities, overhead cost is applied to each event. Large activity costs are broken down to remove any non–value-adding activities that result in process cost savings.

Defects per unit (DPU) is an additional quality measure used to determine how defect-free the items or services being produced are. DPU is a less complicated measure than parts-per-million or six-sigma calculations. This measure aims directly at what customers demand: a defect-free product. It is usually not important to most customers how many problems are occurring or how deep the defects are in a particular product or product line, as would be calculated using ppm or six-sigma methodologies (where products are designed to be twice as good as specifications). Customers simply want defect-free products in the shortest possible time that will fulfill their needs. DPU measures work well in administration and service areas as well as in production areas.

Eliminating defects results in high speed processes, which reduces total throughput time. It means that materials spend less time in queues and storage (waiting) with less paperwork, less to analyze, less to repair, and faster customer response time, resulting in more satisfied customers (see Figure 8.8).

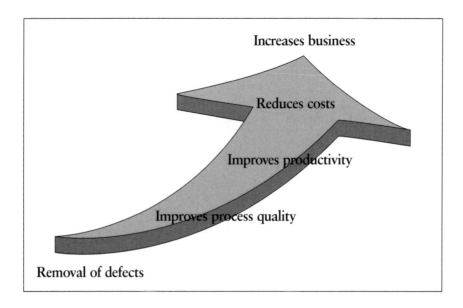

Figure 8.8. Most businesses focus on increasing business when they should focus on removing defects.

MEASURING DEFECTS PER UNIT

To find defects per unit, follow these four basic steps.

1. Determine the product or service you want to measure for defects.

2. Count the total number of units produced during a specified time period.

3. Count the total number of defects or mistakes made during the same time period.

4. Using these data, divide the results from step 3 by the results from step 2. Chart the results using a bar or line graph, showing how far you are from zero (see Figure 8.9).

For example, assume that 2500 reports were produced during the month of March and a total of 45 defects were found and reported by customers. 45 divided by 2500 equals 0.018, which is plotted along with data from other months. This measure will enable you to determine the defect rate trend (see Figure 8.9).

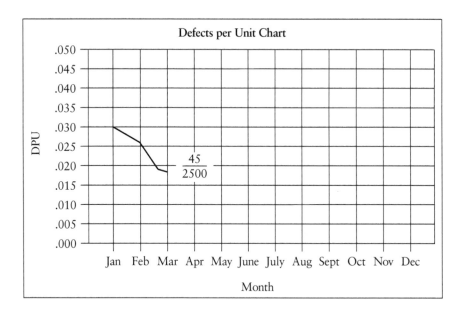

Figure 8.9. Charting defects per unit.

CALCULATING DEFECTS PER UNIT FOR THE DELI CONTRACT

During the process of reviewing the flows at the deli, all employees were asked to put a check mark next to any observed process problems or defects created during their day's work. We established that a defect for the deli operation was anything that had to be done over. The five most common defects identified were made into a check sheet. Any additional errors would be added to the bottom of the list.

1. Order received wrong from a customer.

2. Wrong food ordered from the preparer by the counter person.

3. Wrong food or drink picked up from the waiting counter.

4. Wrong food prepared by the preparer.

5. Order entered wrong into the cash register.

Over the next several days, 1000 orders were processed and the frequency tally totaled on the check sheet (see Figure 8.10). Using these four steps, let's calculate the defects per unit for the deli operations. The total number of units produced was 1000 customer orders. During the processing of these 1000 orders, 67 errors were observed. To determine the defects per unit, the total errors made (67) would be divided by the total number of orders processed (1000), or 0.067 defects per customer order.

Defect type	Frequency tally	Total
Orders received wrong from a customer.	7HL ////	9
Wrong food ordered from the preparer.	7HL 7HL ////	14
Wrong food or drink picked up.	7HL 7HL 7HL /	16
Wrong food prepared by the preparer.	7HL ////	9
Order entered wrong in the cash register.	7HL 7HL 7HL ////	19
		67

Figure 8.10. Check sheet for the deli.

Inputs from Suppliers, Outputs to Customers. There are many ways to look at and measure these kind of data. Customers and suppliers can be internal or external, ultimate or obvious end-users, or hypothetical. Data can be measured by asking common-sense questions: Are we receiving defect-free information, data, parts, products, or services from our suppliers? Have we been trying to make good items using poor supplies? It is usually impossible to produce a defect-free item using inferior inputs, unless costly extra effort is put into the process. It is helpful when analyzing these data to remember the definition of customers and suppliers: *A customer is anyone who receives something, and a supplier is anyone who provides something.*

Direct Customer Feedback and Communication. Since everything begins and ends with the customer, it is mandatory that feedback and communication loops exist so that you can make informed decisions about the ability of your processes to meet your customers' requirements. This has traditionally been done in most businesses by setting up a customer service department. Unfortunately, this type of process usually produces an untimely delay in communicating the problems back to the people producing the products or performing the services.

A lot of energy and resources are wasted dealing with problems at this stage. The ultimate goal is to improve products and services such that there is limited need for a customer service department. Idealistic? Not if you gain complete control of your processes and people are trained in zero-defect methodologies. Feedback loops enable problems to be treated as "treasures"—rare finds or insights that can be used to your advantage for change and improvement. It means focusing on the process instead of the person when a problem occurs (see Figure 8.11). Find out why the process documentation produced something wrong, then correct it.

UNDERSTANDING CUSTOMER NEEDS

Every function, department, and group within a company or organization exists to fulfill a customers' needs, whether they are the ultimate, obvious,

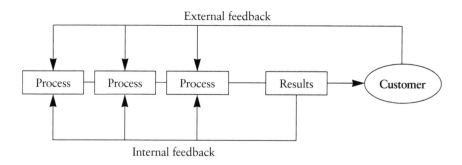

Figure 8.11. Internal and external feedback loops.

or end customer, or an intermediate or internal customer. Those needs will be strikingly similar no matter who the customer is. Once this is understood, it will become easier to start improving your processes.

As we have said before, there is more opportunity to improve processes with internal customers than in trying to increase sales to ultimate customers. You must sell a lot more product to increase profits from sales by 10 percent than if you improved internal processes by 10 percent. You will eventually have to grow your business once processes are improved internally. That will be your next challenge.

Each function, department, group, or organization acts as a supplier when providing an output (information, data, material, product, or service) to a customer. To do this, however, each in turn must have its needs fulfilled by its suppliers. Understanding these organizational, interdepartmental cross-functional needs leads to everyone's fulfillment and makes the processes work, improving productivity. There must be continual interaction and communication between each provider and receiver to discuss needs. Everything you do is included in a chain of cross-functional interdepartmental interactions and should be documented and continuously analyzed for improvement. The goal is to not pass problems downstream to someone else. The ultimate goal is zero defects. The customer survey questionnaire is a valuable tool to determine customer needs and satisfaction (see Figures 8.12 and 8.13).

CUSTOMER SURVEY QUESTIONNAIRE

SUPPLIER INFORMATION:

Department or Company Being Surveyed: _____ Date of Survey: _____

Information, data, material, product, or service provided: _____

_____

_____

SPECIFIC CRITICAL CUSTOMER REQUIREMENTS FOR WHAT IS BEING PROVIDED:

	SCCR	Definition of Requirement	Measures
1.	_____	_____	_____
2.	_____	_____	_____
3.	_____	_____	_____
4.	_____	_____	_____
5.	_____	_____	_____

CUSTOMER RESPONSE: Please review all data on sheet (front and back). When you have contact with the people in the above department or company, how satisfied are you that they . . .

Please circle the number that best describes your level of satisfaction.

	Not Applicable	Very Dissatisfied	Dissatisfied	Satisfied	Very Satisfied
1. Provide the correct information, data, materials, product or service..........	0	1	2	3	4
2. Listen to your suggestions	0	1	2	3	4
3. Take the initiative to help you, or if unable to, will find help	0	1	2	3	4
4. Provide information requested or answers questions quickly..............	0	1	2	3	4
5. Find solutions to your problems	0	1	2	3	4
6. Acknowledge mistakes and takes responsibility for fixing their process	0	1	2	3	4
7. Deliver on time, per expectations	0	1	2	3	4
8. Follow up with you to make sure you are satisfied, asks for feedback...............................	0	1	2	3	4
9. Overall, how satisfied are you with the quality of the information, materials, data, products or services received?..............................	0	1	2	3	4

©1993 Caravatta & Associates 21691 NW West Union Road Hillsboro, Oregon 97124 (503) 647-2841

CSQ - 001   (Continued on the reverse side)

Figure 8.12. Customer survey questionnaire, side 1.

What do you particularly like about the information, data, material, product or service you receive from the above department or company? _____

_____

_____

_____

_____

What do you think could improve the information, data, material, product or service you receive from the above department or company? _____

_____

_____

_____

_____

What information, data, materials, products or services do you receive from the above department or company that you do not need? _____

_____

_____

_____

_____

_____

Additional Comments:

_____

_____

_____

_____

_____

_____

_____

Person or Department Completing Questionnaire:

_____
(Name Optional)

©1993 Caravatta & Associates 21691 NW West Union Road Hillsboro, Oregon 97124 (503) 647-2841

Figure 8.13. Customer survey questionnaire, side 2.

Involvement and Empowerment. Involvement must be accompanied by empowerment for change and improvement. An example of involvement only would be working within a process or team, seeing a need for change, and communicating it to your manager, supervisor, or quality circle team. The suggestion is reviewed, and a judgment made as to its merits; it's either good or bad. The person suggesting the need is involved, but has no real power to change anything, so the need usually goes wanting or the problem keeps recurring, until it moves up on management's priority list. With empowerment, you or your team are not only involved in suggesting change, but have the power to implement it through participation and consensus with the knowledge that change will occur and will be recognized in a controlled environment.

Traditional management says, "We'll make all the decisions and implement the plans; you simply give us the information." That's not empowerment. If a mistake is made, employees will feel that management caused the error, so management can fix it. Management intent on empowering people says instead, "Tell us what's wrong and how you will fix it, and we'll provide the resources." Empowerment gives people ownership of (responsibility for) the project or process. If a mistake is made, people will intuitively want to correct it.

To empower people, managers must embrace the concepts of leadership. They need to provide associates the means to make small incremental changes, remove activities not essential to their process, and try whatever actions they think will improve the process. The focus can be on saving materials, labor, or time, or on providing a safer environment.

The idea is to encourage all associates to be process simplifiers. To do this, they all must be involved in the process within which they work. All potential non–value-adding activities must be focused on and eliminated. Remember, the real resources are the ideas in people's minds. Focusing on this idea will empower every individual to help realize the potential profits in every business.

OLD VS. NEW MEASURES

Major shifts in measuring business performance are occurring, replacing many traditional methods (see Table 8.1). This is happening because direct labor measures such as efficiency, machine utilization, and productivity can lead to establishing incorrect priorities, overcontrol, and accumulation of excess inventory. New measures include the following:

- *Total head count productivity.* Traditional direct labor measures of employees—efficiency, utilization, and productivity—that promote incorrect priorities, overcontrol, and excessive inventory are being replaced by total head count productivity. This is calculated by

Table 8.1. Shifts in measuring performance.

Old Measures	New Measures
Direct labor	Total head count productivity
• Efficiency • Utilization • Productivity	$\dfrac{\text{Output}}{\text{Number of people}}$
Machine utilization	Return on assets (ROA)
	$\dfrac{\text{Net income}}{\text{Total assets (including inventory)}}$
Inventory turns	Days of inventory
Cost variances	Product cost versus competitors
Performance to schedule	Meeting customer requirements • Internal and external • Accuracy • Timeliness • Responsiveness
Promotion based on seniority	Promotion based on skills and process knowledge
Employee involvement • Number of suggestions submitted • Number of suggestions okayed • Number of suggestions implemented	Employee empowerment • Number of ideas generated per person • Number of ideas implemented • Total throughput time • Defects per unit • Number of customer complaints • Response-to-complaint time

dividing the total output dollars, or items produced, by the total number of all production, administration, and service people. This can be done on a weekly, monthly, or yearly basis, and provides a useful picture of a company's overall performance.

- *Return on assets.* Machine utilization, where each individual machine's productivity is measured in isolation from the others, is being replaced by an overall view of all assets. Called *return on assets* (ROA), it equals net income divided by total assets including inventory. The old method often resulted in an accountant determining whether a machine is over- or underutilized. As a consequence, the machine was kept busy even if there was no demand for its output. Incorrect output priorities, overcontrol, and excessive inventories are the frequent result. ROA provides an overall measure rather than a per-unit measure.

- *Days of inventory.* Instead of measuring how frequently inventories of products, subassemblies, or documentation turn over, it is better to measure days of inventory: how many days of parts are on hand to make a complete product, not just how many A parts, B parts, or C parts are on hand. The need is for matched sets of parts that can be assembled to completion within a known time frame. Have available only what is needed to fulfill customer requirements.

- *Product cost vs. competitors.* The old cost variance measure is being replaced by comparing your total product cost with that of your competitors. This provides more of a competitive thrust to meet a key customer requirement: the best product for the lowest price. You may have to perform reverse engineering to arrive at your competitors' total component cost.

- *Meeting customer requirements.* The traditional performance-to-a-schedule measurement is being replace by, "Are we meeting our internal customers' and external customers' requirements?" This measure better addresses customers' real expectations. A complete chain of customers and suppliers working within a managed process is needed to fully meet customer requirements.

- *Accuracy and total quality of a product or service.* This is a measure of dependability, reliability, and responsiveness. Dependability means that a product will operate and perform as specified or advertised. Reliability implies that the product not only operates well when new, but that it will continue to do so for a long period of time. This was a new concept for many Western businesses, which were designing products for obsolescence. Responsiveness is how long it takes to receive a product or service once it is ordered. Responsiveness is a cornerstone for future success.

- *Promotion based on skills and process knowledge.* This measure is based on the skills people have learned and the time they have taken to increase their knowledge, rather than how long they've worked. Twenty-five years of the same output is not as valuable as continually improving your skills to increase your output. Experience is still valued and important, but without a constant upgrading of skills and application to processes, it is neither an accurate nor complete measure of a person's performance.

- *Employee empowerment.* This is a new measure that can be based on several parameters: How many ideas have been generated per person or within a work group? How many ideas have been implemented? Employee empowerment can also be measured using total throughput time per process or per product, or in defects per unit produced.

- *Customer complaints.* The goal for this measure is zero. Customers talk about problems to others, who then talk to more people, causing a chain reaction of negatives. The goal is for customers to say, "We never have a problem" or "We had a problem and they took care of it immediately," instead of "We had a problem and were forced to live with it for quite a while." Complaints can also be measured by how fast you are responding to them. Every complaint has a time limit within which it should be addressed before customer dissatisfaction sets in. This can be determined and measured by simply asking customers.

MEASURING WHAT YOU DO

As we have said before, there is a fundamental need to look at everything you do in your business or organization as part of a total process, rather than as separate, silo activities or functions unconnected to others. To do this, you must have a thorough understanding of the needs of your internal and external customers. Everyone upstream in the process must understand the needs of everyone downstream in the process.

Begin your improvement efforts by identifying any areas where you think you can make small-step improvements. This requires, first and foremost, that your processes be documented. Then ask yourself these simple questions.

1. Are any problems passed to me from upstream processes (my suppliers)?

2. Am I passing any problems to someone downstream (my customers)?

3. Why is my process done in this sequence?

4. Is this the way it has always been done?

5. Is any inspection and rework occurring?

6. Are there any queuing times in the process?

7. Can my work be done differently, more efficiently, or in parallel with other work?

Measurements do not have to be complex or difficult. The measures we have presented provide an easy way for everyone to review and analyze their organization's effectiveness. We believe that these measures, used correctly and consistently, will provide the foundation everywhere within your business or organization for improving productivity. You are encouraged to add these measures to everyone's results management system.

CHAPTER 9

CONTINUOUS IMPROVEMENT IN DAILY WORK

AIM OF THIS CHAPTER

Why wait several years for your closed-loop corrective action process to correct your ISO 9000 or QS-9000 quality system problems? The information in this chapter—combined with the principles, practices, and tools discussed in previous chapters—offers a complete set of improvement tools to achieve instant improvement of your documented quality system or current processes.

The five-step procedure can be used without focusing on the broader, cross-functional business relationships of your company or organization. They work best, however, when used to document the many small steps within cross-functional business processes chosen for improvement.

The five-step procedure enables all operational personnel (administration, services, and manufacturing areas) to

1. Analyze their own daily work tasks.

2. Improve communication with direct customers and suppliers.

3 Remove non–value-adding activities that result in simplified processes.

Examples are provided of a worksheet, customer questionnaire, quality function deployment (QFD) matrix, Pareto diagram, and other tracking forms. Use them to manage cultural change and continuously simplify your business systems and daily work processes.

LOOKING AT PROCESSES

Processes should be looked at in three fundamental ways.

1. As *cross-functional* activities where the whole process is managed at a high level, as discussed in chapter 2.

2. As the *daily work processes* of individuals, where employees are concerned with the details of their suppliers (who they receive something from), what they do, and who they are providing something to (as discussed in this chapter).

3. As a *combination of 1 and 2*: cross-functional management of business processes and management of daily work processes to analyze the details of core business processes.

The first view, *cross-functional process management,* will assist you in identifying breaks in the linkages of a total process. This view is seldom taken in companies we have visited. It should be, because there is rarely only one person, department, or function involved in an overall business process. By itself, cross-functional process management will do a poor job of identifying gray areas—steps that are not linked correctly between departments or functions. We have found that understanding daily work activities first makes observing gray areas between departments or functions easier to identify.

The second view, *continuous improvement in daily work,* will enable you to improve your own group's or department's productivity considerably. It will cause you to look for functional or department non–value-adding activities and ways to simplify work. It also bridges communication between your own department and those on each side of you (your direct suppliers and customers). You will begin providing feedback to your suppliers regarding your needs and asking for feedback from the groups or customers to whom you provide information, data, product, or services for further action (see Figure 9.1). This method is

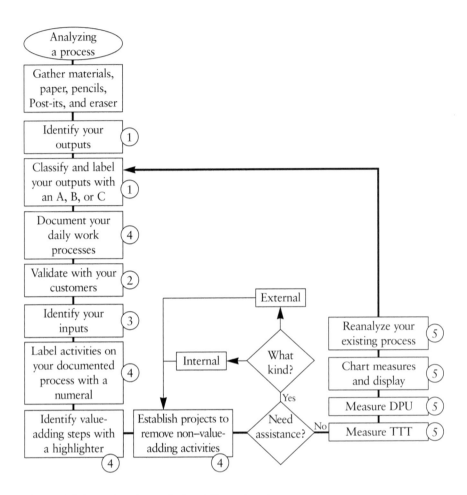

Figure 9.1. Procedure for analyzing daily work tasks.

recommended if cross-functional process management has not been embraced by senior management. It will improve daily task process understanding and assist in removing wasteful activities in a short period of time. The method will not, by itself, address total process issues. Only those issues directly linked to your department documentation or function will be affected.

The third view is a combination of both views that, if implemented jointly, will reduce costs, improve quality, improve flexibility, improve communications, and reduce response time. *The reason I wrote this book is to persuade you to take this view. If you do, cultural change is manageable and the goal of zero defects is achievable.*

Tomorrow's world-class company will be both vertically controlled and cross-functionally process oriented. Neither form will dominate, but processes will be managed with a flatter management structure. Instead of department management, total process management will prevail. Successful core process management will remove much of today's inter-departmental bureaucracy. Executives, managers, and employees will share a feeling of exhilaration, keeping in touch with cross-functional horizontal process changes and knowing that they are made in direct response to internal and external customer needs to increase customer satisfaction (the virtual business).

Change, however, is threatening; therefore, horizontal cross-functional management of processes must be organized to work in concert with existing vertical control structures. Review chapter 2 if necessary.

PROCESS REVIEW EXAMPLE

We will use a real-life example that demonstrates how one task of a building support services person was simplified in a billion-dollar company that was downsizing. Valuable knowledge of processes in this particular administration and services department existed only in people's heads and thus was "walking out the door" as people retired, left, or were laid off. A method was needed to quickly capture and document process information.

The building support services person followed the steps outlined in a pamphlet titled, "Continuous Improvement in Daily Work Processes" (see Figure 9.2). The steps were fully implemented two weeks later and included documented procedures and documented work flows of the new process. The improvement process began with the support person's participation in a Continuous Improvement in Daily Work workshop, which provided the methodology and tools to visually observe, monitor, measure, and improve processes. Knowing that something had to be demonstrated to other workshop participants within two weeks after completion of the

---

Continuous Improvement In
Daily Work Processes

Step 1: **Identify your outputs** – The end results you provide, deliver or communicate to someone else (your customers).

Step 2: (A) **Validate with your customers** – The Specific Critical Customer Requirements (SCCRs) of your outputs, or results listed in Step 1.

(B) **Benchmark others** – Compare your company with, the best practices, methods, services, or products.

Step 3: **Identify your inputs** – The things people (your suppliers) provide, deliver and communicate to you.

Step 4: **Document your daily work processes** – How you currently accomplish work.

Step 5: (A) **Measure Total Throughput Time (TTT)** – How long it takes to produce your output, or end result: information, data, material, product or service.

(B) **Measure defects per unit (DPU)** – Amount of errors or mistakes occurring during your total output.

(C) **Re-analyze your existing processes** – Determine how to remove wasteful activities, calculate their impact.

© 1993 Caravatta & Associates
CIDW - 001

Figure 9.2. Workshop guide cover example.

workshop, a room was reserved to work away from interruptions. Appropriate working materials were gathered (white board, pens/pencils, Post-its, paper, and so on), and the process review steps began.

Step 1a. *Identify your outputs: the end results you provide, deliver, or communicate to someone else (your customers).* This particular person identified three primary outputs that he was responsible for in step 1a: (1) complete minor job requests at lowest possible cost; (2) provide support services on customer requests in the quickest possible time, at the lowest cost; (3) schedule and provide preventive maintenance for buildings 80, 91, and 93 (roofs, floors, walls, ceilings, and doors).

In step 1b, the workshop participant was asked to classify and label each of the related processes identified in step 1a into one of the following categories, using supportive data or facts. If the processes produce outputs or end results that satisfy customers and don't need to be worked on now, assign them an A. If processes produce outputs or end results that aren't working so well, but are acceptable from your perspective, assign them a B. If the processes produce outputs or end results that need to be fixed now, assign them a C. Item 1 was given an A, item 2 a B, and item 3 a B.

Step 2.   *Validate with your customers the specific critical customer requirements (SCCRs) of your outputs or results as listed in step 1.*

Step 2a.   *Select one of the Cs you labeled in step 1b. If you didn't have any Cs, select a B. If no Bs, select an A.* One A and 2 Bs were assigned. The task this person decided to analyze for improvement was item 2, "Provide support services on customer requests in the quickest possible time, at the lowest cost." When asked what this really meant, he discussed how conference room reservations were handled and audiovisual equipment provided for meetings. "I'm tired of constantly being interrupted while performing my other support responsibilities."

Step 2b.   *Complete the top of the customer survey questionnaire:* the sections labeled *department/company being surveyed* and *date of survey* (see Figure 9.3).

Step 2c.   *Document the measures you are using today regarding your selected output or end result in step 1.* Write your measures in the space for SCCRs on the customer survey questionnaire.

Step 2c1. *In the first column, list the SCCRs requested by your customers today.* Three specific SCCRs were listed: (1) available AV equipment; (2) correct room setup; and (3) necessary information or customer requirements understanding.

Step 2c2. *Define the requirements that will deliver each identified SCCR.* Item 1's definition was "per customer needs"; item 2's definition was "per customer request"; item 3's was "per documented requests."

Step 2c3. *What measures will make sure customers receive what is expected?* Item 1's measure was "Is it in the room or not in the room?" Item 2's measure was "Is the room prepared properly or not prepared for meetings?" Item 3's measure was "Are all customer requests documented correctly or incorrectly?"

Step 2d. *Perform the customer survey in person if possible, clarifying any questions as they occur. If unable to conduct the survey in person, use the phone or mail.* Customers' perceptions are recorded on the rest of the survey questionnaire. The customer survey is used to gather information from the people who received the support services. The questionnaire lists all the SCCRs and enables customers to rank their satisfaction or dissatisfaction with the services provided. As you can see on Figures 9.3 and 9.4, there were many dissatisfied customers.

Step 2e. *Note any discrepancies between your assumptions and customers' expectations, and obtain mutual agreement.* You may have to set up a meeting time or conference call to share differences. Negative responses should be treasured; you are being provided improvement areas that will streamline your processes.

Step 2f. *Document and monitor your survey progress using the key customer survey tracking chart* (see Figure 9.5).

CUSTOMER SURVEY QUESTIONNAIRE

SUPPLIER INFORMATION:

Department or Company Being Surveyed: _Support Services_   Date of Survey: _October 1_

Information, data, material, product, or service provided:

Reservations for the Auditorium and conference rooms.

SPECIFIC CRITICAL CUSTOMER REQUIREMENTS FOR WHAT IS BEING PROVIDED:

SCCR	Definition of Requirement	Measures
1. _Available AV equipment_	_Per customer needs_	_In room — not in room_
2. _Correct room set up_	_Per customer request_	_Prepared — not prepared_
3. _Necessary information_	_Documented requests_	_Everything correct — incorrect_
4. _____	_____	_____
5. _____	_____	_____

CUSTOMER RESPONSE: Please review all data on sheet (front and back). When you have contact with the people in the above department or company, how satisfied are you that they . . .

Please circle the number that best describes your level of satisfaction.

	Not Applicable	Very Dissatisfied	Dissatisfied	Satisfied	Very Satisfied
1. Provide the correct information, data, materials, product or service...........	0	1	②	3	4
2. Listen to your suggestions	⓪	1	2	3	4
3. Take the initiative to help you, or if unable to, will find help	0	1	2	③	4
4. Provide information requested or answers questions quickly.............	0	①	2	3	4
5. Find solutions to your problems	0	1	②	3	4
6. Acknowledge mistakes and takes responsibility for fixing their process	0	1	②	3	4
7. Deliver on time, per expectations	0	①	2	3	4
8. Follow up with you to make sure you are satisfied, asks for feedback................................	0	①	2	3	4
9. Overall, how satisfied are you with the quality of the information, materials, data, products or services received?................................	0	①	2	3	4

©1993 Caravatta & Associates 21691 NW West Union Road Hillsboro, Oregon 97124 (503) 647-2841

CSQ - 001   (Continued on the reverse side)

Figure 9.3. Customer survey questionnaire, side 1.

What do you particularly like about the information, data, material, product or service you receive from the above department or company?

Quick response time when something is wrong.

What do you think could improve the information, data, material, product or service you receive from the above department or company?

They need to understand what the customers needs are up front!

What information, data, materials, products or services do you receive from the above department or company that you do not need?

Lack of room preparation, available equipment, working equipment.

Additional Comments:

Why don't you prepare a checklist of information and questions to ask people wanting to reserve a room?

Person or Department Completing Questionnaire:

Marketing, John ext. 7734

(Name Optional)

©1993 Caravatta & Associates 21691 NW West Union Road Hillsboro, Oregon 97124 (503) 647-2841

Figure 9.4. Customer survey questionnaire, side 2.

Customer	Customer contact	Surveyed • In person • By phone • By mail	Dates for survey		
			Started	Completed	Agree
Larry Anderson	Gary Baker	In person	8/96	8/96	Yes
Sam Bell	Gary Baker	In person	8/96	8/96	Yes
Nancy Bell	Gary Baker	In person	8/96	8/96	Yes

Figure 9.5. Key customer survey tracking form.

Step 2g.   *Benchmark others: Compare your company with the best companies in terms of practices, methods, services, or products.* The following suggestions will help make benchmarking activities successful.

a. Make sure you understand the purpose of why you are beginning a benchmarking study.

b. Involve only the best performers in your benchmarking team.

c. Identify what operations, companies, or businesses will become your benchmarking partners.

d. Know your own processes, products, or services before getting to know what others are doing. Know how to answer the questions about your processes that you ask on your questionnaire.

e. Don't become enamored with numbers. You are looking for processes and methods to use.

f. Make sure peer-to-peer exchanges take place (comparing like details to like details).

g. Make sure something happens with the data once they are gathered.

h. Celebrate anything learned and achievements made.

Step 2h. *Use matrices to translate customer requirements into infor-mation, data, materials, products, and services.* The matrix assists in answering the following questions: What are our customer requirements? How are they achieved? How are you doing today? What are your strengths and weaknesses? How much are you doing today? What areas do you need to improve?

There are several ways you can benchmark others' activities, identified in steps 2h1 and 2h2.

Step 2h1. *Compare the incremental small steps you documented (see step 4) with someone else's process' small steps.* Select the best processes discovered and implement them into a revised process.

Step 2h2. *A QFD table was used to identify strengths and weak-nesses compared with two competitors.* Develop a QFD table using the following steps.

a. Identify the *what* items that you would like to improve. In this example we will be improving conference room preparation elements: understanding requirements, quick response time, a prepared and ready room, and equipment that works. Locate the *what* items on the matrix (see Figure 9.6).

b. Rank the *what* items by asking your customers which are the most important to them. In this matrix, 4 has the highest ranking.

c. Break the *what* items down further into one or more *how* items. In this example the *how* items are: ask questions, reserve room, make sure the AV equipment is in the room, inform customer that everything is okay, equipment works, room is set up, and overheads will be visible. These are a further definition of the *what* items. Locate the *how* items on the matrix.

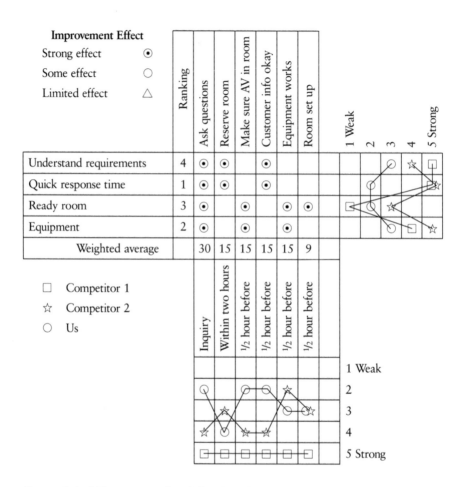

Figure 9.6. QFD matrix to identify benchmarking activities.

d. Use the symbols in the top, upper-left corner titled Improvement Effect to define your perception of the relationships between the *whats* and the *hows*. If no relationship exists, the matrix space is left blank. The interrelationships between the two sets of items point to opportunities for improvement. Notice that no symbols were used other than "strong effect."

e. Calculate the weighted average factor for each *how* item. Strong effect items carry a weight of 3 points, some effect 2 points, and limited effect 1 point. Add the sum of each column together after multiplying by the rating factor. The first weighted average is 4×3 or 12, plus $1 \times 3 = 3$, plus $3 \times 3 = 9$, plus $2 \times 3 = 6$, or a total of 30 for "ask questions;" "reserve room" is $4 \times 3 = 12$, plus $1 \times 3 = 3$ or a total of 15; "make sure AV in room" is $3 \times 3 = 9$, plus $2 \times 3 = 6$, or a total of 15; "customer information okay" is $4 \times 3 = 12$, plus $1 \times 3 = 3$, or a total of 15; "equipment that works" is $3 \times 3 = 9$, plus $2 \times 3 = 6$, or a total of 15; "room set up" is $3 \times 3 = 9$. Ask questions to make sure the correct information is gathered. This carries the most weight.

f. On the bottom of the matrix, list the *how much* items. *How much* items are measurements for the *how* items and provide means for ensuring that requirements are met. *How much* items should be measurable; *how* items aren't usually defined enough. Measures cause actions to occur.

g. Competitive assessment graphs provide an item-by-item comparison between similar competitive products or services. Begin with the graph displayed on the vertical axis to the right of the whats. Discuss techniques with other areas or businesses that provide the same or similar services or products. You are trying to identify who is using the best business processes in their organization. Mark their responses in the competitive assessment section between weak and strong performance using the key listed on the matrix items, 1 thru 5. Do the same for the *how much* items listed.

h. After identifying best practices, you must exchange information, process data, and so on, then integrate them into your processes.

Step 3.   *Identify your inputs,* the things people (your suppliers) provide, deliver, and communicate to you. Use the following steps to identify and track critical inputs on the form for tracking critical inputs needed from suppliers (see Figure 9.7).

a. List the description of the end result you selected in step 1.

b. List your inputs, needs, and requirements to create that end result.

c. List from where and whom your inputs come.

d. Define the specific requirements, elements, features, or measurements necessary to fulfill your needs (you are the receiver or customer).

e. Discuss any disparities with each supplier until a mutual agreement is reached.

f. Document and monitor progress with suppliers using the form for tracking critical supplier needs (see Figure 9.8). This tracking form is used when interfacing with suppliers

Description of end result	Inputs, end results needed from suppliers	Where and whom inputs come from (supplier)	Specific requirements, elements, features, or measurements
Set up room	½ hour before need	Project manager	Type of room setup
Prepare AV equipment	Type of equipment needed	Project manager	Equipment known/works
AV repair	Repair items/parts	Receptionist	Lead time to repair

Figure 9.7. Tracking critical inputs needed from suppliers form.

Supplier	Supplier contact	Discussed • In person • By phone • By mail	Needs discussion date		
			Started	Completed	Mutually agree
Project coordinator	Jo Arnold	In person	8/96	8/96	Yes
Receptionist	Kathy Cook	In person	8/96	8/96	Yes

Figure 9.8. Tracking of critical supplier needs form.

to document your critical inputs. The most important column on the form is the one on the right. It ensures that your primary suppliers agree with you regarding supplier requirements. Register the supplier titles, supplier contacts, how the survey is being conducted, the date started, and the date completed. The mutually agreed on section will either be completed by you while you are discussing the listed elements in person, or by phone, or by the supplier if it is mailed. When conducting the survey in person or by phone, ask suppliers to review the supplier information you entered on the form. Make sure you both agree with these measurements before proceeding.

Inputs regarding this improvement project were received from project managers, schedulers, and the building receptionist concerning the type of room setup, equipment, and lead times.

Step 4. *Document your daily work processes* to trace how you currently accomplish work.

a. Use standard symbols to document your process. Identify the beginning and ending of your process with an oval. Identify all process steps with a rectangle. Identify all decision/action points, where questions are asked, with a diamond.

b. For reference, use a numeric to label each activity on your documented process. These numerics will be used in a future step to measure and establish throughput times.

c. Identify all value-adding steps in your process with a highlighter. The remaining steps are all candidates for removal.

d. Return to step 2 to determine necessary customer requirements. A flowchart was constructed showing all the current steps (today's process) required to set up a room for use. The flowchart visibly displayed many inefficient activities and rework loops (see Figure 9.9).

e. Establish projects to remove all non–value-adding steps such as inspections, rework, and storage: (1) Identify all actions and defects in the process; determine where on the flowchart you will gather error data (measurements). Typically a decision or question symbol (diamond) is displayed on your process flowchart; step 9 in Figure 9.9 was used as the data-gathering point. Work to remove decisions or actions (questions) in your processes. (2) Gather a frequency tally of errors or problems by first listing the types of actions or defects that are made, then tallying their frequency as problems occur during the production process. (3) At the end of a given time period, count the frequency total of each action or defect made. To verify that the count is accurate, count the frequency tally check marks and make sure the number in the total column matches it. Total errors for this particular process were 39 (see Figure 9.10). (4) Prepare a Pareto diagram of your tally, a priority based on facts. Data measured in steps 5a and 5b were presented using the Pareto principle (see Figure 9.11). A chart was constructed displaying errors made in the

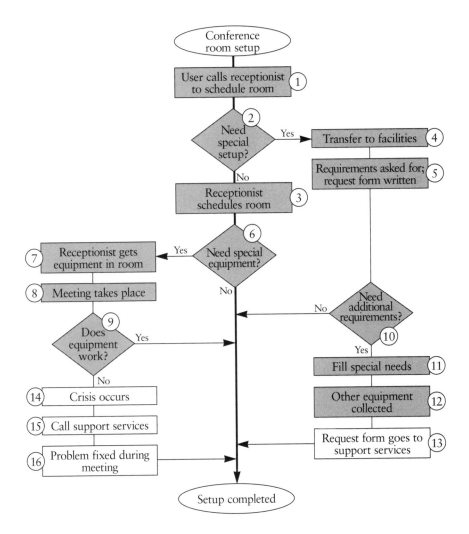

Figure 9.9. Current auditorium setup procedure.

month of August. Notice the types of actions/defects that were grouped into three specific categories: AV (1, 2, 3, 4), conference room setup (5, 6, 7), and receiving the correct data from the customer (8, 9, 10). The Pareto diagram visually displays AV equipment as the biggest problem.

Type of action/defects	Frequency tally	Total
1. Overhead not working	𝑇𝐻𝐿 𝑇𝐻𝐿 ///	13
2. 35 mm projector remote lost	//	2
3. Sony projector not ready	//	2
4. Portable TV/VCR problem	𝑇𝐻𝐿	3
5. Wrong room configuration	𝑇𝐻𝐿 //	7
6. Projection screen up	//	2
7. People wait for room setup	//	2
8. Microphone not set up	//	2
9. Room too small	////	4
10. Setup time too short	//	2
	Totals 39	39

Figure 9.10. Frequency tally of errors.

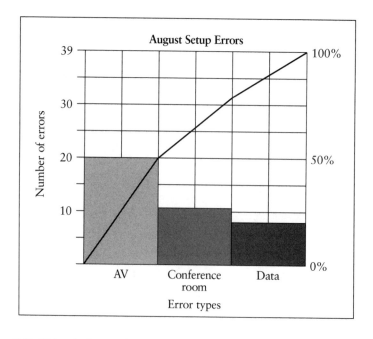

Figure 9.11. Using the Pareto diagram to focus on August error types.

Step 5. *Measure total throughput time.* Mark how long it takes to produce your output, or end result; information, data, material, product, or service. Use the numbered symbols on the original flow diagram established in step 4, activity b. Measure with a stopwatch and record the actual time necessary to perform each step and write the average on the flowchart. Be sure to measure the process routing enough times to establish the true flow paths used. Three process flows were discovered for this process. The first followed steps 1, 2, 3, and 6, taking a total of 3.5 minutes to perform; the second (the most repeated or common process) followed steps 1, 2, 4, 5, 10, 11, 12, and 13 and took an average of 66 minutes; the third followed steps 1, 2, 3, 6, 7, 8, 9, 14, 15, and 16, taking 69 minutes. Review your recorded times and circle those taking the longest time to perform. Analyze the small steps involved in the circled process step and remove any non–value-adding, wasteful activities from it.

a. Measure defects per unit. Record the amount of errors or mistakes occurring during your total output. Total errors were tabulated in step 4e3. The total number of times the room was set up during a one-month period was 49, and the total number of problems identified by customers was 39. DPU was calculated to be 0.796 (39 divided by 49).

b. Reanalyze your existing processes. Determine how to eliminate wasteful activities and calculate the impact of proposed changes. Draw a revised flow of a possible new process. Measure the anticipated revised flowchart's total throughput time on another throughput measurement sheet. Compare your new throughput time with the original time recorded. The original process throughput averaged 66 minutes, while the new process averaged 28 minutes; this is a 38-minute reduction. After the new process was implemented and the kinks removed, it was documented with a process map identifying the necessary steps for secretaries and receptionists to follow (see Figure 9.12). A check sheet (form) incorporating all the critical elements necessary to reserve conference rooms and floor arrangements is shown in Figures 9.13 and 9.14. After the new form was implemented, customers were again surveyed to review the results of the improved process. Feedback results from the new survey indicate improved customer satisfaction (see Figures 9.15 and 9.16).

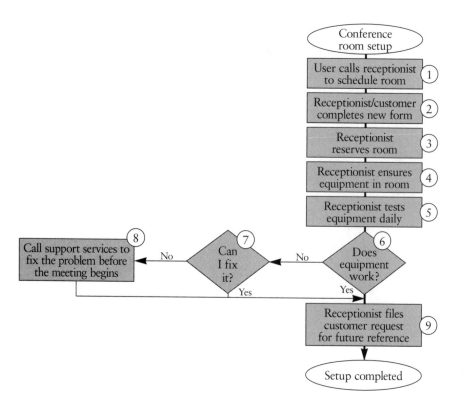

Figure 9.12. Improved auditorium setup procedure showing elimination of steps.

Auditorium Setup Questionnaire

Please complete and return to the building receptionist.

Requestor: *Mary Lou*

Phone number: *685-2803*

Delivery station: *0-301*

1. Date and time of meeting: *October 5*

2. Name of user: *John Kirkwood*

3. Telephone number: *685-2345*

4. Number of attendees: *42*

5. Seminar/meeting name: *Sales briefing*

6. What setup is needed? (standard setup is 125 chairs)
   If special chair/table setup is required, use the diagram on back.

7. Do you need special power setup? (Note on back diagram)

8. Do you need AV equipment? *No* Training to use it? *No*
   a. Overhead ✓
   b. 35 mm projector
   c. Sony projector
   d. Television/VCR ($^1/_2''$ or $^3/_4''$)
   e. Projector screen ✓
   f. Microphone

9. Do you need any of the following? *Yes* Training? *No*
   a. Flip chart or chalkboard ✓
   b. Cable TV
   c. PC-to-TV projector
   d. Teleconference hookup

Figure 9.13. Auditorium setup procedure form.

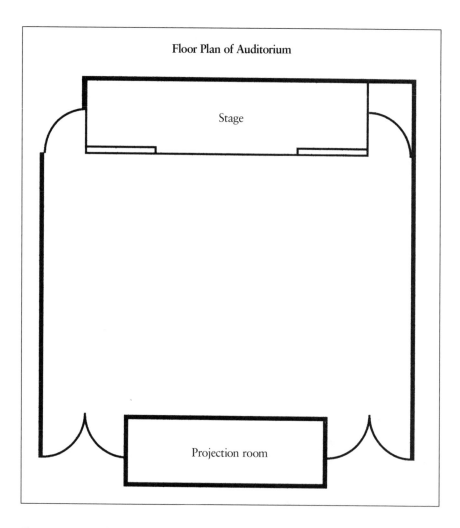

Figure 9.14. Auditorium floor plan.

CUSTOMER SURVEY QUESTIONNAIRE

SUPPLIER INFORMATION:

Department or Company Being Surveyed: *Support Services*   Date of Survey: *October 15*

Information, data, material, product, or service provided:

Reservations for the Auditorium and conference rooms.

SPECIFIC CRITICAL CUSTOMER REQUIREMENTS FOR WHAT IS BEING PROVIDED:

SCCR	Definition of Requirement	Measures
1. *Available AV equipment*	*Per customer needs*	*In room — not in room*
2. *Correct room set up*	*Per customer request*	*Prepared — not prepared*
3. *Necessary information*	*Documented requests*	*Everything correct — incorrect*
4.		
5.		

CUSTOMER RESPONSE: Please review all data on sheet (front and back). When you have contact with the people in the above department or company, how satisfied are you that they . . .

Please circle the number that best describes your level of satisfaction.

	Not Applicable	Very Dissatisfied	Dissatisfied	Satisfied	Very Satisfied
1. Provide the correct information, data, materials, product or service..........	0	1	2	(3)	4
2. Listen to your suggestions	0	1	2	3	(4)
3. Take the initiative to help you, or if unable to, will find help	0	1	2	3	(4)
4. Provide information requested or answers questions quickly.............	0	1	2	3	(4)
5. Find solutions to your problems	0	1	2	3	(4)
6. Acknowledge mistakes and takes responsibility for fixing their process	0	1	2	(3)	4
7. Deliver on time, per expectations	0	1	2	3	(4)
8. Follow up with you to make sure you are satisfied, asks for feedback...............................	0	1	2	3	(4)
9. Overall, how satisfied are you with the quality of the information, materials, data, products or services received?...............................	0	1	2	3	(4)

©1993 Caravatta & Associates 21691 NW West Union Road Hillsboro, Oregon 97124 (503) 647-2841

CSQ - 001   (Continued on the reverse side)

Figure 9.15. New customer survey questionnaire, side 1.

What do you particularly like about the information, data, material, product or service you receive from the above department or company?

Rooms for meetings are well prepared.

What do you think could improve the information, data, material, product or service you receive from the above department or company?

They have improved their services in the last month, congratulations.

What information, data, materials, products or services do you receive from the above department or company that you do not need?

Everything is okay.

Additional Comments:

Your checklist is great!!!

Person or Department Completing Questionnaire:

Marketing, John ext. 7734

(Name Optional)

©1993 Caravatta & Associates 21691 NW West Union Road Hillsboro, Oregon 97124 (503) 647-2841

Figure 9.16. New customer survey questionnaire, side 2.

FOLLOW-UP

A very important part of any improvement effort is to establish a procedure for making sure people do what they say they will do. Too many times I have seen process improvement projects started but never completed due to many and varied factors. Usually, however, the root cause was a lack of complete follow-up by the company's or organization's management to ensure project completion.

■ ■ ■

A large company conducted workshops on project management for more than 7000 people during a five-year period. We later observed that few projects were actually managed with the process, because the company did not have a follow-up program in place to see if people were actually using the learned techniques. Millions of dollars were spent with little documented return to the company. A follow-up process could have ensured that improvement techniques and processes were used and that there was an economic benefit to the company.

■ ■ ■

It is also important that techniques learned to simplify processes be applied in a relatively short time after a learning experience (ideally, within three to seven days). Research has shown that if newly learned techniques are not used within several weeks, they will usually not be used at all. Immediate and visible results are essential to achieve success in any change or improvement process.

Management must become involved in the projects organizational people are working on. This can be accomplished by monitoring projects and ensuring that people are working on the projects they're supposed to be working on. Keep everyone working on improving something! Remember that what gets reviewed and measured usually gets improved.

Problem suggestion	Date documented	Assigned to	CLCA number	Implementation date

Figure 9.17. Problem/suggestion board.

An effective management tool to track projects is a simplified what-are-you-working-on project board mounted on a department wall for all to see (see Figure 9.17). It's a simple, visible display of what is being planned, what is being worked on, and the implementation date.

■ ■ ■

Brian Usilaner (1993), in an article entitled "What's the Bottom-Line Payback for TQM?" states that "many current attempts at implementing TQM strategies fall short of expectations because most of the efforts lack a comprehensive approach to continuously improving quality. People focus only on those criteria with which they are the most comfortable or have existing experience with. They are not changing their existing culture, systems, and processes to sustain a quality improvement strategy. To fully integrate quality strategies into company systems and processes, organizations must place a heavy emphasis on managing their human resources."

■ ■ ■

IN CLOSING

A question was posed to Norman Bodek, president and founder of Productivity Press of Portland, Oregon, by Jeremy Green (1993) for the *Oregon Quality Initiative Quarterly Newsletter.* He asked why it was that many U.S. companies that had started TQM or other continuous improvement efforts within the last five years had failure rates quoted in the press at 90 percent to 95 percent. Bodek's response was, "I think all of us know why they fail. As with anything else, you fail if you don't stay with it. You must stay with it by practicing, learning, and reading. Be willing to have failures, but learn from them."

It is important to not only make sure people apply what they learn in seminars or workshops, but make sure that they keep at it by continually looking for more improvement opportunities in their daily work processes. Most large accomplishments are achieved in small-step increments. You must approach improvement as one would build a brick wall: one improvement at a time.

We'd like to share with you some anecdotes and insights picked up at different locations throughout the world.

- *From workshop participants in Singapore:* There's a story of a small village's residents that did not cook pigs before eating them. One day, a mischievous child accidentally set fire to a barn with a pig inside, and villagers poking around in the embers discovered a new delicacy! This led to a rash of barn fires. The moral: When you don't understand the process, you can "burn down a lot of barns" trying to accomplish something. You should understand the processes you commonly use.

- *From workshop participants in Oregon:* Change is like rainfall: Everyone knows it's necessary but nobody likes to get wet! Once you decide, however, that change is necessary for improvement, DWYSYWD: do what you say you will do! We often say, "this is what we will do," but it doesn't happen.

- *From workshop participants in Washington:* When skiing, keep your skis pointed in the same direction. Focus your human resources on your company's mission, goals, and objectives.

- *From workshop participants in California:* The legendary golfer Ben Hogan said, "If winning is being lucky, the more you practice, the luckier you get." Improving cross-functional processes and daily work tasks becomes easier the longer you work at it.

- *A similar thought was given to me at a workshop in England:* A taxi driver was stopped by a lad carrying a tennis racket. The lad asked the taxi driver, "How do you get to Wimbledon?" The taxi driver responded, "Practice, practice, practice."

I hope that this book inspires you to achieve competitive excellence. Global market competition is upon us and ever increasing; businesses and organizations no longer have the luxury of maintaining old cumbersome styles. I believe that everyone needs to learn to manage cross-functional processes and the individual daily work tasks within them. That is the best way to develop strong alliances between customers, suppliers, and operational personnel. I would like to leave you with these guiding principles.

1. Abandon fixed thinking about daily tasks. Even if things are working well, try to improve them constantly.

2. Carry on innovation at all times. You do not need a problem to make things better. Establish stretch goals for greater achievement.

3. Implement cross-functional process management. Processes within any business or organization are related in some way. Find out how, and manage them!

4. Document your present situation, analyze it, and find a way to simplify work tasks.

5. Think in terms of being both a customer and a supplier in everything you do:

   —You are a customer when you receive materials, information, data, products, or services from an internal or external source.

—You are a supplier when you provide materials, information, data, product, or services to others.

—Look for opportunities between customer and supplier relationships to improve customer satisfaction.

6. Do not seek perfection right away. Progress is made in small-step increments.

7. Remember that mistakes are not problems or defects, as long as you correct them before passing the product or service downstream.

8. Ask the question "Why?" five times and seek true causes.

9. Use brainstorming to utilize the thinking of all knowledgeable people, rather than relying on single sources of information.

10. Executing change is a continuous learning effort.

You've just completed the first step in excelling at executing successful change. Drive your organization to new heights, now! The rewards are yours; don't procrastinate.

AN INVITATION

In our quest for continued learning about executing change and the journey to do so, we invite you to send us stories describing your experiences and insights about executing change. Send your comments to

The Executing Change File
E-mail: Caravatta@aol.com

Michael Caravatta
Caravatta & Associates
21691 NW West Union Rd.
Hillsboro, OR 97124

Services Available

Caravatta & Associates is a consulting and training services company for executing change in the areas of building shared vision, continuous improvement in daily work, teamwork, total quality management, statistical process control, just-in-time manufacturing, material management methods (MRPII), and project management.

254 EXECUTION: HOW TO DO IT!

"Building Shared Vision" and "Continuous Improvement in Daily Work" are the latest in a long line of commonsense workshops that Caravatta & Associates have made easy to understand and accessible to both the public and private sectors.

Caravatta & Associates offers training, speaking services, consulting, and printed material designed to enhance individual and organizational learning and change. We have hands-on experience, files, and tools that often allow us to perform an assignment better and faster than businesses can on their own.

To learn more about how Caravatta & Associates can assist you, your associates, and your organization, please call or write

Caravatta & Associates
21691 NW West Union Rd.
Hillsboro, OR 97124
Phone: 503-647-2841
Fax: 503-647-1225

GLOSSARY

activity-based costing—The gathering of cost information by breaking overhead into cost drivers that determine the final cost of an operation.

activity-based management—The combination of activity-based costing and removing non–value-added operations.

administration—Any function within a company or organization that performs a service to other areas within the company, or to external customers, that is not part of the manufacturing process.

bar chart, bar graph—A pictorial graph made up of vertical or horizontal bars, used to show data plotted against time or amount. Makes data easier to understand.

benchmarking—Continuous comparison of your products, services, practices, and processes with those of industry leaders and applying the findings to improve your company's performance.

brainstorming—An idea-generating technique that uses group interaction to generate many ideas in a short period of time. No limits are usually applied as to what can be suggested or discussed.

bureaucracy—A method for transforming people's energy into wasted effort that hinders progress.

business process—Any activity consisting of a number of steps that must be followed in order for a business to function and meet customer needs. Processes cross over many departments, functions, and groups.

business process analysis—A systematic method to study how work is accomplished in order to find areas for improvement.

CEDAC—Cause-and-effect diagram with the addition of cards, used to resolve problems by reviewing their causes and the effect that their removal has on the end result.

check sheet—A form for tallying how frequently different events or phenomena occur.

commitment—Being emotionally motivated and enthusiastic about goals, projects, and the direction of efforts.

communication—The sharing of thoughts, ideas, perspectives, and feelings; listening to others.

conflict—(during teamwork) A situation where people on the same team have different overall goals.

consensus—An agreement by all team members to support a decision on a specific issue. Not a vote or unanimous agreement.

continuous improvement (CI)—Adopting a mind-set that all things can always be improved, whether problems are occurring or not.

continuous process improvement (CPI)—Same mind-set as CI, and focusing on and monitoring processes to determine if: (a) they are functioning as desired, and (b) they can be improved. CPI requires an attitude of never being satisfied with the existing process.

core process—A process that addresses a major business need; a key core process consists of a group of related tasks in different departments each using resources together to supply an end result.

cross-functional management—The establishment of permanent total process owners for those functions that cut laterally throughout a business or organization; encourages interdepartmental functions to carry out their respective responsibilities with an eye toward downstream departments.

cross-functional processes—Activities that are linked between various functions, departments, or groups.

customer—The recipient or beneficiary of the output of work effort, or the purchaser of products or services. May be either internal or external to the company.

customer/supplier linkages—The relationship that exists when a customer receives an item from an upstream process supplier, adds value to it through a work process, and passes it (as a supplier) to another customer downstream.

cycle time—Time between completions; a measure of how frequently an item comes out of the end of a process.

defects per unit (DPU)—Total number of defects made divided by the total number of items produced.

Deming circle—Plan-do-check-act, the four phases of continuous quality improvement advocated by Deming: plan for improvement (plan), implement improvement (do), analyze the results (check), and take action on the results (act). Abbreviated *PDCA*, this control cycle is a cornerstone of total quality management (TQM).

Deming, W. Edwards—Father of the industrial revolution in Japan. Deming advocated quality and productivity improvement through process control. The prestigious Deming Award in Japan is named after him.

downstream customers—People, functions, departments, or groups that receive products or services from a providing supplier in a process.

empowerment—Providing people with the tools and authority/responsibility to implement process change and improvement through participation and consensus. Requires that people believe that process change will occur, take an active part in change, and will be recognized in a controlled environment.

event—An observable action or evidence of a problem.

executing change—Integrated methodologies for implementing continuous process improvement throughout businesses and organizations. Focuses on strategic change, defining and documenting cross-functional processes, defining and improving relationships and linkages between internal customers and suppliers, documenting individual daily work processes, and simplifying productivity measurements. Emphasizes total employee involvement and empowerment, elimination of non–value-adding activities, maximum cross-functional communications, and teamwork. Puts in place a single productivity program for all.

facilitate—To manage, articulate, or influence a process, project, people, or activity to achieve a desired end result or improvement.

fail-safe—Within processes, fail-safe methods are those that prevent defects or mistakes from occurring.

"fear factor"—(within companies and organizations) The fear of losing your job. It manifests itself as an uneasiness that people show when unsure about what is expected of them, or what management will do to them if/when they make a mistake. Fear in the workplace almost always makes people counterproductive in improvement efforts.

feedback—An integral part of any working system, consisting of the data or information received by a supplier from a customer (internal or external) about how expectations and needs are being met.

fiefdom—see *bureaucracy.*

"find-and-fix"—A method of using quality tools to detect problems and correct them, to bring a process back to where it was originally.

flowchart—A chart that symbolically shows work or process movement and direction as a series of steps. A general example would be input from suppliers, value-adding work activities, and output to customers. A visual method of documenting all processes.

follow-up—Refers to the discipline required to make sure that agreed-on plans and changes are being implemented and new processes and procedures are used and followed.

functional organization—An organization responsible for one of the major corporate business functions such as marketing, sales, engineering, design, production, processing, finance, and distribution.

goal—Desired future condition, including measurable end results to be accomplished within specified time limits.

gray area—The confusion or uncertainty that exists between functions involving customer/supplier handoffs in a horizontal process. A key part of business processes that is often ill-defined and managed.

histogram—A frequency distribution represented in the form of a vertical bar chart.

horizontal organization—The process structure that must be managed across the traditional vertical organizational structure. Involves linking all the process steps used in completing one process within functions, departments, or groups.

horizontal process—A series of activities or tasks that must cross interdepartmental boundaries to be completed.

hoshin kanri—A methodology to integrate an organization's strategic quality planning (medium-term to long-term visions and goals) with all of its business processes and daily work activities. In Japanese, *hoshin* is generally translated as "direction or policy," while *kanri* means "management or control." Hoshin planning is a broad concept that aims at helping pull together all departments or functions within a company and uniting the minds of the people to prevent problems from being passed to downstream processes. (In the United States, the words are often used to refer to *management by process*, a system of management control techniques based on the principle of eliminating waste and conflict from internal processes.)

improvement—Within a business, an increase in productivity, profits, and morale. A belief that there is no such thing as status quo—things are either improving or getting worse. Changing a process to make it more efficient and to enhance its value.

innovation—The introduction of something new; to make changes; a new idea, method, or device.

input—Materials, energy, data, information, products, or services received from others (suppliers) and used to complete daily work tasks. Can be internal or external to the company.

inspection—Comparison of an end result to a standard.

invisible inventory—Any support functions characteristic of service groups—marketing, engineering, administration, sales, distribution, finance, information systems, and so on—that are invisible.

ISO 9000 quality system documentation standards—International Organization for Standardization standards for a quality assurance system. Accepted internationally, the ISO 9000 series specifies what process documentation for quality assurance must be in place and how it must be followed. The standards do not make any value judgment as to the documentation being right or wrong, nor do they specify how to achieve quality.

kaizen—Japanese word implying gradual, unending improvement. Continually trying to do every little thing better. Setting and achieving ever-higher standards.

"killer" phrases—Words or statements that can inhibit or stop the flow of ideas by causing people to hold back or give up altogether.

leadership—Positive behavior that displays the ability and willingness to conceptualize and articulate goals, create confidence, show support, promote change for improvement, coach and facilitate, and create and maintain a positive environment.

Malcolm Baldrige National Quality Award (MBNQA)—Award criteria that have been selected to help raise quality performance standards and expectations; facilitate communications and the sharing of key quality and operational performance requirements; serve as a tool for planning, training, and assessment; and continually improve value to customers.

management control (vs. self-control)—The establishment of processes for employees to succeed. Making sure the discipline exists to follow procedures.

measurement—The act or process of obtaining achieved results for comparison to requirements.

method—A way, technique, or process for doing something.

methodology—A body of practices, procedures, and underlying principles used to deploy a discipline.

objective—A statement of action to reach a desired future condition or goal. It includes measurable end results to be accomplished within specified time limits.

output—Materials, energy, data, information, products, or services provided to others (customers) used to complete daily work tasks. Can be internal or external to the company.

overhead—The cost of doing business: accounting, engineering, marketing, sales, and so on. Variable overhead is the overhead that could be eliminated if a process is improved (for example, floor space, heat, and so on).

Ps, the five—

- *Passion*—Show high enthusiasm for improving people, processes, and procedures. Continuous display of improvement interest, ideas, efforts, and results.

- *Provide*—Give people information and the freedom to use it.

- *Patience*—Provide the time necessary and the encouragement for improvement efforts to succeed. Understanding that real improvement must be a long-term, continuously strived-for goal.

- *Persistence*—Continuously encouraging change and improvement.

- *Publicize*—Providing recognition of change. Encouraging everyone to get on the bandwagon: Get people saying "What do I need to do?" or "How can I get involved?"

paradigm—Set of rules and regulations that describe the boundaries of a job, task, organization, activity, and so on that tells you what to do within those boundaries.

paradigm shift—Changing to a new set of boundaries, with a new set of rules.

Pareto chart—Vertical bar chart showing the distribution of factors contributing to a problem or situation in descending order from the left to right. Distinguishes the vital few from the trivial many. Used to prioritize improvement efforts.

Pareto principle—Used as a prioritizing tool to determine what to work on and what actions will have the greatest impact based on occurrences. You will get an 80 percent improvement by attacking the critical 20 percent of existing problems. Conversely, you will get a 20 percent improvement by attacking the remaining 80 percent of existing problems. Named after Vilfredo Pareto, who observed a mathematical proportional relationship between the vital few and the trivial many, whether considering products, ideas, or problems.

PDCA—Plan, do, check, act. The traditional business control cycle that lies at the heart of total quality management (TQM). Originally proposed by W. Edwards Deming and Walter Shewhart in 1946 (see also *Deming circle*).

poka-yoke—Japanese word meaning "prevention of defects." Equivalent to the Western term "fail-safe." Those methods or techniques added to processes to prevent defects or mistakes from occurring (see also *fail-safe*).

procedures—Documentation of all the specific steps or tasks supporting a process. (The ISO 9000 series standards call them "work instructions."

process—A series of actions by which something is produced and passed from one condition, person, department, group, or function to another. A set of interrelated work activities that are characterized by receiving inputs and adding value to produce a desired output.

process control—Making sure that processes are documented and followed.

process criteria—The review and measurement of all criteria used to produce products or services.

process improvement—Changing a process to make it more efficient, to enhance its value to the company or organization in terms of customer satisfaction and needs fulfillment.

process map—A flowchart that traces the actual movement of information, data, materials, products, or services within the work environment.

process owner—The coordinator of all activities, at all levels of a process. Manages the process from end to end to ensure overall optimal performance.

project schedule plan—The steps a team develops to implement a solution or actions needed to improve or manage a process or project.

"pronoun" test—Asking frontline workers a few general questions about the company or organization and listening to the pronouns they use. Usage of "they" or "them" means it is one kind of company, "we" or "us" means it is another kind of company.

QS-9000 requirements—Quality system requirements developed for the automotive industry that consist of ISO 9001 with some additional requirements.

quality—The ability of a product or service to meet the needs and expectations of the customer. What the receiver (customer) says it is.

quality excellence—Implemented in the early 1920s and 1930s by Henry Ford and Walter Shewhart of AT&T. Stresses continuous improvement in daily work and the elimination of waste.

quality function deployment (QFD)—The use of matrices to compare all elements of a business or organization.

reject—The loss of labor or materials resulting from defects that cannot be repaired or used.

responsibility matrix—Identifies who is responsible for given tasks in a project schedule plan.

results criteria—The measurement of past performance criteria. Emphasizes controls, performance, results, and rewards or nonrewards. The Western style of management recognizes results criterion exclusively.

rework—A process to correct defects produced within a process.

Ss, the five—

- *Seri*—Sort; get organized
- *Seiton*—Simplifying; put things in order
- *Seiso*—Shining; cleaning up
- *Seiketsu*—Standardization; establish standard procedures
- *Shitsuke*—Self-discipline to follow the procedures

SDCA—Standardize, do, check, act. Refinement of the business control cycle PDCA, where standards, once established, become the starting point.

self-check—Inspecting your own work so that you will not pass a defect downstream.

self-control (vs. management control)—Knowing what you are supposed to be doing and doing it. Following established procedures.

service—Any function within a company or organization that provides something to other areas within the company, or to external customers, that is not part of the manufacturing process.

shadowing—Following another employee to observe what he or she does in daily work task(s).

silo effect—A condition that occurs when functions, departments, or groups are working independently of others. Each group plans and manages its own activities and competes for company resources and recognition, impeding productive cross-functional activity and total business processes.

standardization—Choosing the best method of doing things to enable employees to perform their jobs successfully and maximize productivity.

standards—Policies, rules, or procedure guidelines that result from standardization.

statistical process control (SPC)—The application of statistical methods to analyze a process, data, or a study.

storage—The time that elapses when a product or service is between processes or waiting.

supplier—The provider of a product or service; may be either internal or external to the company or organization.

system—Process controls applied to ensure that a process is operating efficiently and effectively.

teamwork—More than two people working together to improve processes, with a willingness to accept the following:

- Support group goals as individual goals.
- Trust other team members and be honest with them.
- Recognize when other team members need assistance and assist them.
- Provide a supportive environment for new process ideas.

throughput time—The time between when a task gets started until it is completed in one function, department, or group (see also *total throughput time*).

total quality management (TQM)—An integrated effort at improving everything at every level in an organization. Activities must include or consider everyone in the company or organization: top management, middle management, supervisors, all other employees, outside suppliers, vendors, and customers. Referred to as *total quality control* in Japan.

total throughput time (TTT)—A measure of the total time from the beginning of all cross-functional, interdepartmental, horizontal activities until all supplier activities have been completed for one task.

transformation—The processing of information, data, materials, products, or services into end products.

transportation—Activity that occurs when a product is moved or changed in location or position.

value-adding—Performing an activity that a customer will willingly pay for.

variation—A comparison against specifications; the difference between actual and identified goals.

vertical organization—Company or group organizational structure that flows from top to bottom in a pyramid shape, usually indicating lines of reporting authority.

visible inventory—Inventory that is traditionally associated with businesses producing hard goods—raw materials, supplies, and finished products—that can be seen.

visible management—Providing instructions and information about the elements of a job in the form of charts, graphs, pictures, videotapes, and other visual aids so that employees are able to maximize their performance.

vision—A picture of a future state for the business, organization, or functional department. A description of what it will look like a number of years from now; a commitment.

Ws, the five, and an H—*Who, what, where, when, why,* and *how* questions used to organize data to solve problems.

waste—Any part of a process where resources are expended that do not add value to the final product or service. This typically occurs during inspection, testing, transportation, and storage. Waste occurs during the handling of items, the generation of unused reports, all forms of rework, and producing anything that ultimately becomes scrap. More familiar examples of waste include inaccurate data, late deliveries, warranty expenses, excessive lead times, and excessive inventory.

world-class—Exceptional performance. The best among global competitors. Producing a product or service that can compete in the global marketplace. Being world-class is increasingly dependent on meeting certain criteria such as international quality standards (ISO 9000), zero defects, continuous process improvement, and having a continuous innovation process.

zero defects—Products or services completely free of variation with full conformance to requirements.

BIBLIOGRAPHY

Akao, Yoji. 1991. *Hoshin Kanri: Policy Deployment for Successful TQM.* Portland, Ore.: Productivity Press.

Annual Productivity Survey. 1991. *Modern Materials Handling* (February).

Beckhard, Richard, and Wendy Pritchard. 1992. *Changing the Essence: The Art of Creating and Leading Fundamental Change in Organizations.* San Francisco: Jossey-Bass Publishers.

Bhote, Keki R. 1987. *Supply Management: How to Make U.S. Suppliers Competitive.* New York: American Management Association.

Caravatta, Michael. 1992. "Continuous Improvement in Daily Work." In *Proceedings of the 9th International Conference on Total Employee Involvement.* Portland, Ore.: Productivity Press.

Covey, Stephen R. 1989. *The Seven Habits of Highly Effective People.* New York: Simon & Schuster.

Crosby, Philip B. 1979. *Quality Is Free.* New York: McGraw-Hill.

Deming, W. Edwards. 1986. *Out of the Crisis.* Cambridge, Mass.: MIT Center for Advanced Engineering Study.

Executives Say Business Process Reengineering Will Change Radically. 1995. *Quality Progress* 28, no. 11 (November): 18.

Fukuda, Ryuji. 1983. *Managerial Engineering*. Portland, Ore.: Productivity Press.

GAO. 1991. *Management Practices*. GAO/NSAID-91-190. Washington, D.C.: U.S. General Accounting Office.

Gardner, Howard. 1996. *Leading Minds: An Anatomy of Leadership*. New York: Basic Books.

Goddard, Walter E. 1986. *Just-in-Time: Surviving by Breaking Tradition*. Essex Junction, Vt.: The Oliver Wight Companies.

Goldratt, Eliyahu M., and Robert E. Fox. 1986. *The Race*. Milford, Conn.: North River Press.

Green, Jeremy. 1993. *Oregon Quality Initiative Quarterly Newsletter* (fall): 1.

Hanan, Mack. 1985. *Consultative Selling*. New York: American Management Association.

Harrington, H. James. 1991. *Business Process Improvement, The Breakthrough Strategy for Total Quality, Productivity, and Competitiveness*. New York: McGraw-Hill.

Hielsen, Greg. 1991. *Meta Business: Creating a New Global Culture*. Reno, Nev.: Conscious Books.

Huge, Ernest C., with Alan D. Anderson. 1988. *The Spirit of Manufacturing Excellence: An Executive's Guide to the New Mindset*. Homewood, Ill.: Dow Jones-Irwin.

Imai, Masaaki. 1986. *Kaizen: The Key to Japan's Competitive Success*. Portland, Ore.: Productivity Press.

Ishikawa, Kaoru. 1983. *Guide to Quality Control*. Tokyo: Asian Productivity Organization.

Kouzes, James M., and Barry Z. Posner. 1987. *The Leadership Challenge: How to Get Extraordinary Things Done in Organizations*. San Francisco: Jossey-Bass.

Lowenthal, Jeffrey N. 1994. Reengineering the Organization: A Step-by-Step Approach to Corporate Revitalization, Part 1. *Quality Progress* 27, no. 1 (January): 93–95.

Machiavelli, Niccolò. 1961. *The Prince*. New York: Grove Press.

Managing Amid Chaos. 1993. *FORTUNE*, 5 April.

Mizuno, Shigeru. 1988. *Management for Quality Improvement: The 7 New QC Tools*. Portland, Ore.: Productivity Press.

NIST. 1993. *Quality Pays* (brochure). Gaithersburg, Md.: National Institute of Standards and Technology.

———. 1997. *Malcolm Baldrige National Quality Award 1997 Criteria for Performance Excellence*. Gaithersburg, Md.: National Institute of Standards and Technology.

Ohno, Taiichi. 1988. *Workplace Management*. Portland, Ore.: Productivity Press.

Peters, Tom. 1992. *Liberation Management: Necessary Disorganization for the Nanosecond Nineties*. New York: Random House.

Popplewell, Barry, and Alan Wildsmith. 1990. *Becoming the Best: How to Gain Company-Wide Commitment to Total Quality*. Carol Stream, Ill.: Hitchcock Publishing.

Rummler, Geary A., and Alan P. Brache. 1990. *Improving Performance: How to Manage the White Space on the Organizational Chart*. San Francisco: Jossey-Bass, 1990.

Senge, Peter M. 1990. *The Fifth Discipline: The Art and Practice of the Learning Organization*. New York: Doubleday Currency.

Shingo, Shigeo. 1986. *Zero Quality Control: Source Inspection and the Poka-Yoke System*. Portland, Ore.: Productivity Press.

———. 1987. *Key Strategies for Plant Improvement*. Portland, Ore.: Productivity Press.

Shinohara, Isao. 1988. *NPS New Production System: JIT Crossing Industry Boundaries*. Portland, Ore.: Productivity Press.

Sontag, Harvey. 1989. *Corporate Perceptions: A Quality Primer.* Milwaukee, Wis.: ASQC Quality Press, 1989.

Suzaki, Kiyoshi. 1987. *The New Manufacturing Challenge: Techniques for Continuous Improvement.* New York: Free Press.

Usilaner, Brian. 1993. What's the Bottom-Line Payback for TQM? *Engineering Management Journal* 5 (June).

Wilson, Harry W. 1994. *Keep It Simple.* Beaverton, Ore.: Begin Publishing Company.

Wright, Russell O. 1990. *A Little Bit at a Time: Secrets of Productive Quality.* Berkeley, Calif.: Ten Speed Press.

INDEX